Dimensions of Motivation and Leadership in Insurance and Banking Sector
(A Comparative Perspective)

Dimensions of Motivation and Leadership in Insurance and Banking Sector

(A Comparative Perspective)

P. Konda Reddy
T. Vijaya Kumar
G. Haranath

GRP

GLOBAL RESEARCH PUBLICATIONS

NEW DELHI (INDIA)

First Published - 2010

ISBN: 978-81-89630-03-4

Published by

GLOBAL RESEARCH PUBLICATIONS
4830/24, 1st Floor, Ansari Road
Darya Ganj, New Delhi-110002 (India)
Phone : 23245225. Fax : 91-11-23272135
E-mail: serials@satyam.net.in

CONTENTS

CONTENTS

PREFACE

The present study brings out the dimensions of motivation and leadership in Insurance and Banking sectors in Nellore district of Andhra Pradesh. Chapter one briefly discusses the various dimensions of motivation and leadership. Chapter two reviews the literature on motivation and leadership and research design. Chapter three shows the amalysis of motivation in select branches of Insurance and Banking sectors. Chapter four analysis the leadership styles followed in Insurance and Banking sectors. Chapter five discusses the subordinates perception of leadership styles of superiors in Insurance and Banking sectors. Chapter six analyses the difference of leadership styles followed in Insurance and Banking sectors. Chapter seven brings out the impact of leadership on motivation in Insurance and Banking sectors. Chapter eight presents the summary of findings and conclusions.

ACKNOWLEDGEMENTS

At the out set we wish to express our profound gratitude and deep respect to our research supervisor Prof. K.Seshaiah (Retd.), for his scholory guidance, affectionate encouragement in carrying out our research work. Inpsite of his multifarious commitments he took keen interest in our work and offered many valuable suggestions in the preparation of the thesis. Words are therefore inadequate to express our sense of gratitude to him.

We feel extremely grateful to Sri Anam. Sanjeeva Reddy, Sri Anam Vivekananda Reddy, M.L.A., Secretary and Correspondent, S.V.G.S. College, Sri A. Chandra Sekhar Reddy, Member, S.V.G.S. College, Nellore for their affectionate blessings and encouragement. And we express our sincere thanks to Dr. Ch. Mohan Reddy, Principal, Sri Ch. Narayana Reddy, Librarian, Sri K.V.S.D.P.V. Prasad, lecturer in Statistics, S.V.G.S. Degree College and Sri T.V. Ashok Kumar Reddy, Principal, S.V.G.S. Junior College, Nellore who has encouraged us to carry on work.

We would like to express and heartful thanks to Sri A.L.Narasimha Rao, Lead District Manager, Sri Y.V.N. Krishna Murthy, Steno to D.M, Syndicate Bank, Nellore, Sri M.V. Siva Prasad, Officer, Sri G. Srinivasa Murthy, C.R.O., Andhra Bank Nellore, Sri P.Sudhakar, Asst., S.B.I., Nellore, Sri B Muralidhar, H.G.A. L.I.C., Nellore, Divisional Office, Nellore, Sri T. Shamsheere, Development Officer, C.B - II, L.I,C., Nellore, Sri G. Venkateswarlu, Asst. L.I.C, Kavali, Sri K. Lalithamma, H.G.A., L.I.C., Gudur and Sri C.N. Murthy, Development Officer, L.I.C., Naidupet for their invaluable help during the period of data collection. We fail if we could not express our thanks to all the sample respondents without whose valuable co-operatioin this endeavour could not have been success.

P. KONDA REDDY
T. VIJAYA KUMAR
G. HARANATH

LIST OF ABBREVIATIONS

L.I.C.	—	Life Insurance Corporation of India.
C.B.B.	—	Commercial Bank Branches.
et. al.	—	and others.
P.	—	Page
P.P.	—	Pages.
Vol.	—	Volume
Ed.	—	Edition.
N.	—	Number of samples
X	—	Mean.
S.D.	—	Standard deviation.
SEOP	—	Socio Economic organisation position.
Viz.,	—	Namely.
Higher level	—	Higher Level Executives
Middle level	—	Middle Level Executives
Lower level	—	Lower Level Executives
Jr. Manager	—	Junior Manager
Sr. Manager	—	Senior Manager
Asst.	—	Assistant
H.G.A.	—	Higher Grade Assistant
D.T.C. Principle	—	Divisional

1

DIMENSIONS OF MOTIVATION AND LEADERSHIP

Motivation is highly complex as it is related to human beings. Organisations, being social systems, heavily depend on the motivational levels of their employees. However, the complexity of the concept of motivation in terms of its understanding and practice has been increasing day by day with the changes in knowledge and technology. As a result the performance of organizations has a direct bearing on motivation of their employees. Thus, motivation has become to challenging task to the management. In order to overcome the problems of motivating people there has been a greater demand for its understanding. Towards this, the concept of motivation has been explored and theorized by social and behavioural scientists in difference dimensions. As such many theories found their place in the literature on motivation and its related concepts of leadership.

Incidentally, even there has been an overlapping between the concepts of motivation and leadership creating a close knit between them. As the scholars and practitioners have identified separate theories for both motivation and leadership. However the fact remains that the motivation represents to an unmet need which creates stimulus driving towards achieving the state of satisfaction. The duty of the leader is to fulfill the employee needs and influence them towards a common objective with the help of the satisfaction they derive. This chapter attempts to examine different theories of motivation and leadership.

DIMENSIONS OF MOTIVATION

Human motivation is a compound phenomenon. It touches upon the dimensions of both the leadership and personality.

What is motive and what isn't, is indistinguishable. The term motivation is derived from a Latin word "Movere" meaning "to move". Thus, anything which moves an individual into action to actualize something is a motive. Daniel Goleman in his book, "Emotional Intelligence" writes, that "Every emotion is a motive". "All emotions are, in essence, impulses to act, the instant plans for handling like that evolution has instilled in us. The very root of the word 'emotion', is 'to motere'. The Latin verb 'to move', plus the prefix 'e' – is to connote the 'move away' suggesting that a tendency to act is implicit in every emotion". In essence it moves people into action. He points out that the word "Emotion" is derived from the Greeck words for 'to' and 'motion'. Emotion means "to move", 'not to think and then move', just 'to move'. In the light of this meaning, it can be concluded that any need, desire, aspiration idea, ideal, thought, feeling and urge that can drive to detract an individual to generate energy–physical (Body), emotional and intellectual (Mind) and spiritual (Spirit) and spend (Annihilate) for a desired result is a motive. This meaning is evident from the concept of motivation which convey that it is process that starts with a physical or psychological deficiency or need that activates a behaviour or drives that aims at a goal or incentive.

In the words of V.H. Vroom[1] "the term motivation refers to a process governing choices made by persons or lower organisations among alternative forms of voluntary activity".

According to Berelson and Steinner[2] motivation is viewed, "as an innerstate that energizes,activates and directs the behaviour of individuals towards certain goals".

In the words of W.G. Scott[3], "motivation means a process of stimulating people to action to accomplish desired goals".

According to D.E. McFarland[4], "motivation refers to the way in which urges, drives, desires, aspirations, strivings, needs direct control, or explain the behaviour of human beings".

Jones[5] defined, "how behaviour gets started is energized, is sustained, is directed, is stopped, and what kind of subjective reaction is present in the organism while all this is going on".

According to Craig Pinder[6], "work motivation is a set of energetic forces that originate both within as well as beyond an individual's being, to initiate work-related behaviour, and to determine its form, direction, intensity and duration".

According to J.L. Gray and F.A. Starke[7], "motivation is the result of processes, internal or external to the individual, that arouse enthusiasm and persistence to pursue a certain course of action".

Fred Luthans[8] defines, "motivation is a process that starts with a physiological or psychological deficiency or need that activates behaviour or a drive that is aimed at a goal or incentive".

Obviously the above stated definitions cover all stages in the motivation process.

At different stages in the evolution of management thought, managers are subscribed to different classifications, approaches, models and theories of motivation. According to their evolved order

1. the traditional model;
2. the human relations model; and
3. the human resources model.

The Traditional Model

The traditional model of motivation is associated with F.W. Taylor and the scientific management school. This school held that an important aspect of the manager's job was to make sure that workers perform their repetitive tasks in a more efficient way. This perspective assumed that workers were essentially lazy and that managers understood the worker's jobs better than the workers did. Workers could only be motivated by financial reward and had little to contribute beyond their labour. In many a situation this approach was proved to be effective.

The Human Relations Model

Elton Mayo and other human relations researchers found that the social contacts of employees at work were also important and that the repetitiveness of the tasks was responsible factor in reducing motivation. Mayo and others also opine that managers could motivate employees by acknowledging their social needs and by making them feel useful and relevant. As a result, employees were given some freedom to make their own decisions on the job.

In the human relations model, workers were expected to accept management's authority because supervisors treated them with consideration and were attentive to their needs. The intent of managers, however, remained the same to have workers accept the work situation as established by managers.

The Human Resources Model

McGregor and Maslow and other researchers such as Argyris and Likert, criticized the human relations model as being simply a more sophisticated approach to the manipulation of employees.

From a human resources perspective, the managers should not induce workers to comply with managerial objectives by attracting them with high wages, as in the traditional model or manipulate them with considerate treatment, as in the human relatons model. Instead, managers should share responsibility for achieving organisational and individual objectives, with each person contributing on the basis of his or her interests and abilities.

THEORIES OF MOTIVATION

There are several approaches to the study of motivation. A perusal of the theories will help to understand the nature of motivation better. The major classification of motivation theories, cover (1) 'Content theories' which focus on the 'what' of motivation; (2) 'Process theories' which focus on the 'how' of motivation; and (3) 'Reinforcement theories', which focus on the ways in which behaviour is learnt.

Content Theories

Maslow's need hierarchy theory, Herzberg's two factor theory. Alderfer's ERG theory and McClelland's achievement theories are classified as content theories. One of these are familiar to managers because these authors have strongly influenced the management field and have affected the thoughts and actions of practicing managers.

Process Theories

The process theories of motivation are concerned with answering the questions of how individual behaviour in energized, directed, maintained and stopped. This section examines Victor Vroom's expectancy theory, Adam's equity theory, Porter and Lawler's performance satisfaction theory. Basic to process theories of motivation is the motion of expectancy.

Reinforcement Theories

Reinforcement theories advocated by B.F.Skinner and others, are also often called behaviour modification or apparent conditioning. These theories deal with how the consequences of a past action influence future actions in a cyclical learning process. In this view, people behave the way they do because, in the past, they learnt that certain behaviours were associated with pleasant outcomes and that other behaviours were associated with unpleasant outcomes. Because people usually prefer pleasant outcomes, they are likely to avoid behaviours with unpleasant consequences.

The theories of motivation have also been classified into different groups by different authors. The following are some of such classifications.

Lee[9] Classified Motivation Theories as:

(a) Needs theories (Maslow, McClelland, Atkinson etc.,)

(b) Work environment and work characteristics theories (Herzberg, Hackman and others)

(c) Expectancy/Path goal theories (Vroom, Georgopoulos, etc.,)

(d) Economic theories (Lawler, Porter and others)

Handy[10] *Classified Motivation Theories as:*

(a) Satisfaction theories (Maslow, Roethlisberger, Dickson, McGregor, Herzberg, etc.,)

(b) Incentive theories (Vroom, Llawler, Porter, etc.,)

(c) Intrinsic theories (Maslow, Likert, McGregor, Argyris, etc.,)

(d) Motivational calculus theory (Handy)

From the above all important classifications the following theories are explained.

Hierarchy of Needs Theory

A need hierarchy of five levels by A.H. Maslow[11] has gained wide attention.He hypothesized that within every human being there exists a hierarchy of five needs. These needs are

- *Physiological:* Includes hunger, thirst, shelter, sex and other bodily needs.
- *Safety:* Includes security and protection from physical and emotional harm.
- *Social:* Includes affection, sense of belonging, acceptance and friendship.
- *Esteem:* Includes internal esteem factors such as self-respect, autonomy, and achievement; and external esteem factors such as status, recognition and attention.
- *Self Actualization*: The drive to become what one is capable of becoming; includes growth, achieving one's potential , self-fulfillment.

As each of these needs becomes substantially satisfied, the next need becomes dominant. A substantially satisfied need no longer motivates. So if you want to motivate someone, according to Maslow, you need to understand what level of hierarchy that person is currently on and focus on satisfying those needs at or above that level.

He separated the five needs into higher and lower order. Physiological and safety needs were described as lower-order and social, esteem and self actualization as higher order needs are satisfied internally (within the person) whereas lower order needs predominantly satisfied externally (by such things as money, wages, union contracts and tenure). The conclusion to be drawn from Maslow's classification is that in times of economic plenty, almost all permanently employed workers have their lower-order needs substantially met.

Maslow[12] himself stated that the theory seems, for most people, to have a direct personal subjective plausibility. Yet it still lacks experimental verification and support, I have not yet been able to think of a good way of putting it to the test......

HERZBERG'S TWO-FACTOR MODEL

Another proposition that has become popular with scholars and practitioners is Herzberg's[13] dual factory theory. In brief, the theory propounds that job satisfaction and job dissatisfaction operate on two separate dimensions. The hygiene or maintenance factors which includes pay, status, work conditions, job security and relations act as a curb on job dissatisfaction.

The motivating factors are intrinsic ones such as achievement, recognition, responsibility, the content of work and the possibility of personal growth. These are the factors which contribute to job satisfaction. The empirical data in support of the theory present evidences by Brayfeild and Croket[14].

After reviewing the empirical evidences to test out Herzberg's theory, Dunnett, Campbell and Hackel[15] come to the conclusion that the theory is an oversimplification of the relationships between motivation and satisfaction and the sources of job satisfaction and dissatisfaction. The distinct and the dual categorization between dissatisfiers and motivators as spelled out by Herzberg cannot claim universal application because personal motivation is often complicated by the concreteness of organisational climate found in India. The interplay between dissatisfiers and satisfiers does not make it conceivable that these two categories will make distinct entities with separate identities.

ERG Theory

Clayton Alderfer[16] of Yale university has reworked Maslow's need hierarchy to align it more closely with the empirical research and labled as ERG theory.

He argues that there are *three groups of core needs - existence, relatedness and growth*, hence the lable: ERG theory. The existence group is concerned with providing our basic material existence requirements. They include the items that are physiological and safety needs.

The second group of needs are those of relatedness-the desire we have for maintaining important interpersonal relationships. These social and status desires require interaction with others if they are to be satisfied and they align with Maslow's social need and the external component Maslow's esteem classification. Finally, Alderfer isolates growth need-an intrinsic desires for personal development. These include the intrinsic component from Maslow's esteem category and the characteristics included under self-actualization.

Besides substituting three needs for five in contrast to the hierarchy of needs theory, the ERG theory demonstrates that (1). more than one need may be operative at the same time, and (2). if the gratification of a higher-level need is satisfied, the desire to satisfy a lower-level need increases.

NEED ACHIEVEMENT THEORY OF McCLELLAND

Shortly after world war II, a group of psychologists led by David C. McClelland[17] of Harvard University began to experiment with TAT (Thematic Appreciation Test), has identified three types of basic motivating needs. He classified as *Need for power (n/PWR), Need for affiliation (n/AFF)*, and *Need for achievement (n/ACH)*

McClelland[18] also distinguishes between social power and personal power, depending on the intention of and the purpose for, the use of power. He has sought to establish that the strength of need achievement is the source of entrepreneurial efforts and, as such, such efforts have a direct correlation with economic development. While examining the data presented by McClelland and his colleagues in support of the theory, Lee[19] has quoted with approval from Atkinson et.al[20]

McClelland[21] admits that, some people who have a compelling drive to succeed are striving for personal achievement rather than the rewards of success. They have a desire to do something better or more efficiently than it has been done before. This drive is the achievement need.

The corporate leadership studies in the contemporary USA by Kanter[22], Peters[23], Menzies[24] indicate that more than need achievement, the issue of power, the position in an organisation, and the Achilles Heel caused by uncertainty and unpredectability of business situations put demands on corporate leadership which cannot be understood or explained by need achievement theory.

The third need isolated by him is affiliation. It can be viewed as the desire to be liked and accepted by others. Individuals with a high affiliation motive strive for friendship, prefer cooperative situations rather than competitive ones, and desire relationships involving a high degree of mutual understanding.

VROOM'S VALENCE EXPECTANCY THEORY

Prominent Vroom's[25] model is built around the concepts of value, expectancy and force. According to Vrooms, valence means strength of an individual's preference to a particular outcome. Another factor in determining the motivation is expectancy, that is, the probability that a particular action will lead to the outcome.

The rubic of expectancy, path/goal models of V.H. Vroom[26], is prominent proposition is that a highly motivated producer would desire a reward he visualizes as a result of effort put in and that if he had worked hard enough to produce the result he would have received the reward expected. In this model extrinsic and intrinsic rewards are not differentiated. The motivation to perform at a key level is determined by the person's belief concerning the probability. This belief is conditioned by the person's self-esteem as well as by his previous personal and observed experience in similar and identical situations.

According to Henemen and Schwab[27], opine that empirical research on expectancy indicates that despite the promise of the Vroom model there are a number of unanswered questions such as our lack of knowledge of the variety of goals carrying positive value in work situations for different actors as also the differences in strength which lead to the choice of one goal over another.

EQUITY THEORY

The theory owes its origin to several prominent theorists like Festinger, Heider, Homans, Jacques, Patchen Weick and Adams. But Adams[28], further researched, and formulated this theory which was labeled as Adam's equity theory.

According to Adam's[29] theory individuals compare their job inputs and outcomes with those of others and then respond so as to eliminate any inequalities.

One of the problems is that people may overestimate their own contributions and the rewards others receive. Certain inequities may be tolerated for sometime by employees[30]. But prolonged feelings of inequity may result in strong reactions to an apparently minor occurrence. Again, it is difficult to assess the perceptions and misperceptions of employees. Hence Dunham[31] commented that, although easily understood the theory is complex and difficult in applications.

PORTER AND LAWLER MODEL OF MOTIVATION

Layman W.Porter and Edward E. Lawler[32] have derived a substantially more complete model of motivation and have applied it in their study primarily to managers. They propose a multivariate model to explain the complex relationship that exists between job attitudes and job performance.

The elements of this model is (1) effort (2) performance (3) rewards (4) satisfaction

Lawler[33] believes that motivation to perform is conditioned by the perceived consequences of good performance and also by the person's estimate of the probability that effort can be converted into successful performance. A more limited application of the expectancy theory to productivity movement has been calculated by Georgopoulos et.al[34] with a concept of path-goal. The contemporary organisational realities are so dynamic that such a one-factor approach can have a limited explanatory value.

Handy[35] proposes that motivational calculus is the heart of the problem. Calculus, according to him, is broader than the term "effort" which has been used by Lawler and it has three components: (a) the strength and salience of a need; (b) the expectancy that will lead to a particular result; and (c) the instrumentality of that result in meeting the needs. Thus, there are components of strength, expectancy and instrumentality which constitute the calculus motif. Handy goes on postulating the source of calculation that can emanate from the unconscious as well as from the conscious and, as such, he acknowledges the role of the unconscious in the motivational map unlike many other management theorists.

There is also a reference to the role of self concept or the ego-ideal in the motivational paradigm. All in all, Handy is of the view that each individual possesses a motivation calculus mechanism while engaged in an activity. Handy's proposition does not offer an insight which is new to the previously propounded motivational literature. There are many variables like intra-specific and inter-specific to an economic organisation in relation to its business environment and socio-economic and cultural contexts.

Theory 'X' and Theory 'Y'

Douglas McGregor[36] proposed two distinct views of human beings: one basically negative, labelled theory 'X', and the other basically positive, labelled theory 'Y'.

The management action of directing human beings in the organisation, according to McGregor[37], involves certain assumptions, generalisations and hypotheseis relating to human behaviour and human nature is based on a certain grouping assumptions and that he or she tends to mould his or her behaviour towards subordinates.

Under theory 'X', the four assumptions held by managers are:

(a) Employees inherently dislike work and, whenever possible, will attempt to avoid it.

(b) Since employees dislike work, they must be coerced, controlled or threatened with punishment to achieve goals

(c) Employees will avoid responsibilities and seek formal direction whenever possible.

(d) Most workers place security above all other factors associated with work and will display little ambition.[12]

In contrast to these negative views about the nature of human beings, McGregor listed the four positive assumptions that he called theory "Y":

(a) Employees can view work as being as natural as rest or play

(b) People will exercise self-direction and self-control if they are committed to the objectives.

(c) The average person can learn to accept, even seek, responsibility

(d) The ability to make innovative decisions is widely dispersed throughout the population and is not necessarily the sole province of those in management positions.

McGregor held to the belief that theory Y assumptions were more valid than theory X. Therefore, he proposed such ideas as participation in decision making, responsible and challenging jobs, and good group relations as approaches that would maximise and employee's job motivation.

REINFORCEMENT THEORY

Psychologist B.F.Skinner[38] of Harvard developed an interesting-but controversial-technique for motivation. This approach, called positive reinforcement or behaviour modification, holds that individuals can be motivated by proper design of their work environment and praise for their performance while the punishment for poor performance produces negative results.

Skinner and his followers do far more than praise good performance. They analyse the work situation to determine what causes workers to act the way they do, and then they initiate changes to eliminate troublesome areas and obstructions to performance. Performance improvements are rewarded with recognition and praise. Even when performance does not equal goals, ways are found to help people and praise them for the good things they do.

This technique sounds almost too simple to work, and many behavioural scientists and managers are skeptical about its effectiveness. However, a number of prominent companies have found the approach beneficial[39].

It emphasizes removal of obstructions to performance, careful planning and organising, control through feedback, and the expansion of communication.

Goal-Setting Theory

Edwin Locke[40] placed a Goal Setting Theory a heavy emphasis on internal states. He is the major theorist and researcher in this area, he began his analysis by arguing that there are two cognitive determinants of behaviour : *values* and *intentions* (goals). A value is something the individual acts to gain or keep. Intentions are goals that individuals seek to attain in order to satisfy their desires or emotions.

Specific hard goals produce a higher level of out put than does a generalised goal of "do your best". The Specificity of the goal itself acts as an internal stimulus. Even individuals trying for a goal so high though rarely reach it perform better than those who are attempting to attain easy goals.

A person's goal of performance will, according to Locke, help a manager to predict the person's future performance and satisfactions. Thus, he argues that all other theories of motivation, are insufficient unless they include a goal-setting dimension.

DIMENSIONS OF LEADERSHIP

Leadership means many things to many people. This is due to the changing environment of leaders in different roles in different functions in different settings starting from leadership of the family to the top positions in multinational organizations. However, the essentials of leadership are the same to all leaders in all positions. Nevertheless, due to the variation in the skills required, roles played, functions performed, issues tackled and the relationships promoted, different leaders have had different perceptions of leadership. As such, several attributes have been made both for the success and failure of leadership in the form of properties and processes or traits and styles of leaders. Further, even these attributes cannot provide a totally satisfactory guidance for the success of leadership. Hence, theoreticians and practitioners of leadership have gone to the extent of developing the 'contingency approach', which emphasizes that there is 'No single best way'. The concept of leadership discussed by different writers, researchers and practitioners are presented in the following passages.

CONCEPT OF LEADERSHIP

There are as many definitions of leadership as there are scholars who have attempted to analyze and understand the concept, but there is no universally accepted definition of it[41].

The word 'leader' stems from the root *leden* meaning 'to travel' or 'show the way'. It has been derived from the verb "to lead." This also implies "to advance," "to expel," "to stand out," to guide and govern the actions of others. A leader is a person who leads a group of followers.

The understanding, developing, predicting and managing the behaviour of leaders is still an enigma, despite the fact there are about 33,000 articles and books have been written about so far in 20th century. The basic question is 'what in fact constitutes leadership?' While Gore and Silander[42] have mentioned about five thousand entries on the concept of leadership, Stogdill[43] reviewed seventy two definitions of leadership. Karmel[44] is of the opinion that it is very difficult to settle on a single definition of leadership that is general enough to accommodate these many meanings and specific enough to serve as an operationalisation of the variable. However, there is a certain underlying unity among the various conceptualizations made in this area.

According to *Management Guru*, Peter F. Drucker[45], "Leadership is the lifting of man's visions to higher sights, the raising of a man's performance to a higher standard, the building of a man's personality beyond its normal limitations."

Different scholars have focused on multiple aspects of leadership like: the creative and directive force of morale (Munson[46], 1981); the process by which an agent induces a subordinate to behave in a desired manner (Bennis[47],1959); the presence of a particular influence relationship between two or more persons (Hollander and Jullian[48], 1969); directing and coordinating the work of group members (Fiedler[49],1967); an interpersonal relationship in which others comply because they want to, not because they have to (Merton[50], 1969); transforming followers, creating visions of the goals that may be attained, and articulating for the followers the way to attain these goals (Bass[51], 1985; Tichy and Devanna[52], 1986); the process of influencing an organised group toward accomplishing its goals (Roach and Behling[53], 1984); actions that focus resources to create desirable opportunities (Campbell[54], 1991); the leaders job is to create conditions for the team to be effective (Ginnett[55], 1996); etc. According to Andrew[16] (1998), some view leadership as the personal relationship between the individual and the group; others as the process of striving toward common goals and values; still others, as aspects of behaviour, whether desired and in control of the individual or, alternatively, reactive and driven by forces in the environment.

The common characteristic that can be found in many of the definitions is the 'influence', exerted by the leader. That is, he tries to influence the behaviour of others in a specific direction.

THEORIES OF LEADERSHIP

Leadership has been discussed, analysed and understood from several dimensions.

The varied experiences of people involved in the process through changing times have provided different perceptions of the subject. Consequently theoreticians and practitioners have approached the subject from their own perspectives resulting in many theories of leadership. As a result leadership has come to mean different things to different people in different contexts. Though the idea of leadership has been known from times immemorial and practised, it is in the 20th century that it has been explored/studied in depth and theorized from many angles. Economists, sociologists, psychologists, political scientists, and anthropologists and others have been investigating into the subject. Nevertheless, there has been no consensus among them regarding it except that leadership is the relationship between a leader and his followers. Whatever may be one's position in the organizational hierarchy or institutional context; he guides, directs, or influences others towards specific objectives. However, the controversy relating to leadership regarding its meaning, inputs, processes and outputs and their impact on the motivation of people, organizational performance and executive effectiveness and success, has continued with the result that search for new theories, comprehensive and adequate, too has been going on. Leadership is akin to parental guidance in respect to children. In view of what is expected in respect to individual employee or a group in an organization. Leadership if need be for the performance of activity is to guide the individual or group to go about successfully to accomplish the task entrusted to the people. This kind of leadership may relate to knowledge related to the segments in the operational system and organizational and technical means and methods to be judiciously employed to accomplish the task assigned and specified objectives to be realized.

In simple terms, leadership is the ability to influence a group toward the achievement of a goal. It is essential to business, government and countless groups and organizations that shape the way we live, work and play[57]. The source of influence may be formal, such as that provided by virtue of his position by the manager of an organization or informal as in other social and political organizations.

Approaches to Leadership

From the voluminous literature on leadership three basic approaches can be identified to explain what makes an effective leader. The first approach seeks to find universal personality traits that leaders have and non-leaders do not have. The second approach tries to explain leadership in terms of the behaviour that a person is engaged in. Both approaches have been considered as 'false starts', because they are based on erroneous and over-simplified conceptions[58]. Thus contingency models have been evolved not only to explain the inadequacies of earlier theories but also to identify which of the situational factors is most important for leadership and to predict which leadership style will be most effective in a given situation.

In the early twentieth century with the development of the Scientific Management Movement, increasing emphasis was laid on organizational leadership. F.W. Taylor initiated time and motion studies to analyse work tasks to improve performance in every aspect of organizational functioning. The most notable function of the leader under the Scientific Management or the classical theory was to enhance organizational effectiveness, while the primary aim of the leader was to improve organizational efficiency and not individual efficiency.

In the 1930's Taylor's emphasis was drastically modified by the Human Relations Movement that was initiated by Elton Mayo and his colleagues. Mayo emphasised that for an organization to enhance its effectiveness it has to take into account human feelings, attitudes and processes involving inter-personal interaction. Therefore, in the Human Relations School, the focus of the leader was not only on the development of the organization, but also on the growth of the individuals managing such an organization.

In recent years the assumption of Human Relations Approach has been challenged by a number of researchers like McGregor, Argyris, Schein, Likert, etc., who highlight the Human Resources Approach rather than the over-simplified approach of human relations. This approach views that human beings are influenced by a set of complex and interrelated factors. These factors take into account the enormous talent, and potential that an individual brings to his work-place with him. It is a question or giving him opportunities to utilise his talent, creativity and potentials by giving him a meaningful work assignment and by adding greater responsibility, autonomy, variety, etc.

The theories of leadership can be conveniently divided into three viz., 1. Trait theory 2. Behavioural theory 3. Contingency theory.

TRAIT APPROACH TO LEADERSHIP

Early studies of leadership in the 1940s and the 1950s concluded that leadership is largely a matter of personality, a function of specific traits. A successful leader not only secures the desired behaviour from his followers but succeeds in creating a sense of satisfaction among them. Leadership traits cannot be fixed with certainty for all leaders. But a leader cannot be effective unless he possesses certain basic qualities. The following are some of the studies that attempted to identify these traits:

Ordway Tead[59] has suggested ten qualities of a good leader:

1. Physical and nervous energy,
2. Sense of purpose and direction,
3. Enthusiasm,
4. Friendliness and affection,
5. Integrity,
6. Technical mastery,
7. Decisiveness,
8. Intelligence,

9. Teaching skill, and
10. Faith.

Chester 1. Barnard[60] has indicated two aspects of leadership traits:

1. Commanding subordinates admiration includes outstanding qualities in respect of physique, skill, technology, perception, knowledge, memory and imagination,
2. Individual superiority in determination, persistence, endurance and courage.

Henry Fayol[61] regards the following as the quaiities of a good leader:

1. Health and physical fitness,
2. Intelligence and mutual vigour,
3. Moral qualities,
4. Knowledge, and
5. Managerial ability.

George R. Terrg[62] has suggested the following qualities:

1. Energy-both mental and physical
2. Emotional stability
3. Knowledge of human relations
4. Empathy
5. Objectivity
6. Personal motivation
7. Communication skills
8. Teaching ability
9. Social skills and technical competence.

Stogdill[63] identifies through research the following traits:

1. Physical characteristics such as age, appearance, height and weight;
2. Social background-education, social status and mobility;
3. Intelligence-superior judgement, decisiveness, knowledge and fluency of speech;

4. Personality-alertness, self-confidence, personal integrity, self-assurance and dominance needs;
5. Task related characteristics-high need for achievement and responsibility, initiative and a high task orientation; and
6. Social characteristics.

Keith Davis[64] lists the following as the characteristics of leadership:

(a) Intelligence: Leaders tend to have higher intelligence than their followers.

(b) Social maturity and breadth: Leaders have a tendency to be emotionally mature and to have a broad range of interests.

(c) Inner motivation and achievement drives: Leaders want to accomplish things; when they achieve one goal, they seek out another. They are not primarily dependent on outside forces for their motivation.

(d) Human relations attitudes: Leaders are able to work effectively with other persons. They respect individuals and realize that to accomplish tasks they must be considerate to others.

Leadership Skills

Some researchers have mixed the skills with the traits resulting from the development of human relations by a leader with the subordinates.

Chris Argyris[65] mentions the following characteristics of a leader:

1. The leader is constantly interacting and commanding.
2. The leader makes the organization a part of his self image.
3. The leader's personal goals, values and feeling the organizationally centred.
4. The leader handles the supervisors as individuals.
5. The leader controls the transmission of important information.

6. The leader emphasizes the present.
7. The leader sets realistic goals.

According to Harold Koontz[66], every group of people that performs near its total capacity has some person as its head who is skilled in the art of leadership. This skill seems to be a compound of at least four major ingredients: (1) the ability to use power effectively and in a responsible manner, (2) the ability to comprehend that human beings have different motivation forces at different times and in different situations, (3) the ability to inspire followers, and (4) the ability to act in a manner that will develop a climate conducive to responding to and arousing motivations.

Katz[67], in his classic study of managers identifies three important types of managerial skills: technical, interpersonal, and conceptual. Diagnostic skills are also prerequisites to managerial success.

Technical Skills. These are the skills necessary to accomplish or understand the specific kind of work being done in an organization.

Interpersonal Skills. The ability to communicate with, understand, and motivate both individuals and group.

Conceptual Skills. These depend on the manager's ability to think in the abstract. Managers need the mental capacity to understand the overall workings of the organization and its environment, to grasp how all the parts of the organization fit together, and to view the organisation in a holistic manner.

Diagnostic Skills. These are skills that enable a manager to visualize the most appropriate response to a situation. Successful managers have them.

Gary Yukl[68] (1981) summarising the research in the field till his times, identified following traits and skills as characteristic of successful leaders:

Traits Characteristic of Successful Leaders:

1. Adaptable to situations
2. Alert to the social environment
3. Ambitious and achievement-oriented

4. Asserti ve
5. Cooperative
6. Decisive
7. Dependable
8. Dominant (the desire to influence others)
9. Energetic (high activity level)
10. Persistent
11. Self-confident
12. Tolerant of stress
13. Willing to assume responsibility

Skills Characteristic of Successful Leaders:

1. Clever (intelligent)
2. Conceptually skilled
3. Creative
4. Diplomatic and tactful
5. Fluent in speaking
6. Knowledgeable about the group task
7. Organized (administrative ability)
8. Persuasive
9. Socially skilled

Michael and Dean[69] suggest a number ofleadership skills critical to success in the global economy. They include the following:

I. *Cultural Flexibility.* In international assignments this skill refers to cultural awareness and sensitivity. In domestic organizations the same awareness could be increasing diversity. Leaders must have the skills not only to manage but also to recognize and celebrate the value of diversity in their organizations.

2. *Communication Skills.* Effective leaders must be able to communicate, in writing, orally, and nonverbally.

3. *Human Resource Development (HRD)* Skills. Since human resources are so much a part of leadership

effectiveness, that leaders must have the HRD skills of developing a learning climate, designing training programmes, transmitting information and experience, assessing results, providing career counseling, creating organizational change, and adapting learning materials[70].

4. *Creativity*. Problem solving, innovation, and creativity provide the competItIve advantage in today's global marketplace. Leaders must possess the skills to not only be creative themselves but also provide a climate that encourages creativity and assist their people to be creative.

5. *Self-management of Learning*. This skill refers to the need for continuous learning of new knowledge and skills. In the times of dramatic change and chaos, leaders must undergo continuous change themselves. They must be self-learners.

An academic analysis made by Kanungo and Misra[71] noted "the prevailing conceptualizations of skills required for successful managerial performance hinders our understanding of the phenomenon". To get over this problem, Whetten and Cameron[72] provide a more empirical derivation of effective leadership skills. On the basis of an interview study of over 400 highly effective managers, the following ten skills were identified

I. Verbal communication (including listening)
2. Managing time and stress
3. Managing individual decisions
4. Recognizing, defining, and solving problems
5. Motivating and influencing others
6. Delegating
7. Setting goals and articulating a vision
8. Self-awareness
9. Team building
10. Managing conflict.

Follow-up studies and related research have found skills similar to the ten above.

Through statistical techniques, the results of various research studies were combined into the following four categories of effective leadership skills:

1. Participative and human relations
2. Competitiveness and control
3. Innovativeness and entrepreneurship
4. Maintaining order and rationality[73],

Traits Research and Results

In general, the search for leadership traits has been largely unsuccessful. It has failed to demonstrate a consistent and definite relationship between leadership ability on one hand and physical traits or personality characteristics or a combination of the two on the other[74]. Byrd[75], in a critical assessment of research on Trait theory upto 1940, identified a long list of traits made by studies, which had differentiated between leaders and the led. He found that only 5 per cent of the traits listed in them were common to four or more of the studies. Another study by Jennings[76], concluded: 'fifty years of the study have failed to produce one personality trait or set of qualities that can be used to discriminate between leaders and non-leaders'.

Later studies identified some correlation between leadership and certain personality traits; for example a significant correlation was seen between leadership effectiveness and such traits as intelligence, supervisory ability, initiative, self-assurance and individualitl[77]. A definite correlation was observed in some cases between the traits of intelligence, scholarship, dependability, responsibility, social participation and socio-economic status of leaders, as compared with non-leaders[78]. But even these correlations between traits and leadership are not really pervasive. Most of the so-called traits are in essence the pattern of behaviour that one would expect from a leader, particularly in a managerial position[79].

In general, studies of leader's traits have not been a very fruitful approach to explain leadership. Not all leaders possess all the traits, and many non-leaders may possess most or all of them. Also, the trait approach gives no guidance as to how much of a particular trait a person should have to be a leader. Furthermore, the dozens of studies that have made do not agree as to what traits are leadership traits or what their relationships are to actual instances ofleadership. Most of these so-called traits are really patterns of behaviour.

BEHAVIOURAL APPROACH TO LEADERSHIP

When it became evident that effective leaders did not seem to have any distinguished traits or characteristics peculiar to them researchers tried to isolate the behaviours that made leaders effective. In other words, rather than try to figure out what effective leaders were, researchers tried to determine what effective leaders did-how they delegated tasks, how they communicated with and tried to motivate their subordinates, how they carried out their tasks, and so on. Unlike traits, however, behaviours can be learnt; if followed, therefore, that individual trained in appropriate leadership behaviours would be able to lead more effectively[80].

The following are the important studies, which come under the behavioural approach to leadership.

McGREGOR'S THEORY 'X' AND THEORY 'Y'

This theory is related to both leadership and motivation. From the leadership point of view it emphasizes the assumptions of managers regarding the behavioural patterns of subordinates. From the motivation point of view it provides directions to managers to deal with subordinates of different types as perceived by the managers.

McGregor identified two major perceptual structures which he labelled 'theory X' and 'theory y,[81]. The manager who perceives people according to either structure, regardless of whether or not he recognizes or acknowledges such perceptions, will behave in predictable patterns because of his personal assumptions, beliefs and attitudes.

According to McGregor, the assumptions of a given manager, that may be inferred in his actions, are traced backward from how he must perceive people to cause him to act that way. If he is strongly authoritarian, he insists on giving orders and commands, rather than suggestions and counseling. In this one would predict theory 'x' perceptual structure. The manager who is less aloof; spends time, teaching and training his subordinates emphasizes obtaining resuits rather than following procedures, and delegates authority, shows signs of embracing theory 'y' assumptions. Thus theory 'x' approximates closely to 'authoritarian', and theory 'y' to 'participative' leadership styles of managing. As an addition to 'x' and 'y', theory 'z' has been introduced.

THEORY 'Z'

In contrast to the traditional, more bureaucratic American organization environment, Ouchi[82] recommends a Japanese style Theory 'z' environment. The problem of productivity in the United States will not be solved with monetary policy nor through more investment in research and development. It will only be remedied when we learn how to manage people in such a way that they can work together more effectively.

The Characteristics of Theory 'z' are:

- Long-term, life time-employment;
- Slow process of evaluation and promotion;
- Development of company-specific skills, and moderately specialised career path;
- Implicit, informal control mechanisms supported by explicit, formal measures;
- Participative decision-making by consensus;
- Collective decision-making but individual ultimate responsibility;
- Broad concern for the welfare of subordinates and co-workers as a natural part of a working relationship, and informal relationship among people.

THE LEWIN, LIPPITT AND WHITE STUDY

One of the earliest attempts to delineate the dimensions of leadership behaviour was made by Lewin and others[83]. This research, in addition to triggering off many other studies based on the same model, was also 'picked by managerial practitioners. As a result of their observations of the behaviour of a small group of children in a laboratory situation, the following three categories of leaders were identified.

(a) *The authoritarian leader:* He himself makes all the decisions that relate to the group and is probably the only source of influence in the group's activities. His most effective technique in maintaining this leadership position is by withholding knowledge of goals, not sharing information required for the task, and not providing feedback to members on their progress.

(b) *The democratic leader:* He makes decisions jointly with his subordinates, showing his power and influence with the group. The participative process, although time-consuming, effectively encourages each members input and familiarity with the problem. The leader gains additional information from group members as well as a greater commitment to the decision than that would occur under authoritarian conditions.

(c) *The laissez-faire leader:* He allows subordinates to make all the decision. His role becomes that of a general supervisor who establishes merely the broad policies and outline of things to be done and then delegates the implementation to his subordinates. As the term, 'laissez-faire' implies, such a leader is a figurehead and makes no contribution to the group goal attainment. No direction is given to the group members.

According to their study of Lewin and 'others, the democratic style of leadership is more effective than the other styles.

OHIO STATE STUDIES

The most comprehensive and replicated of the behavioural theories resulted from research that began at Ohio State

University in the late 1940s[84]. These studies sought to identify independent dimensions of leader behaviour. Beginning with over a thousand dimensions, they eventually narrowed the list down to two categories that substantially accounted for most of the leadership behaviour described by subordinates. They called these two dimensions initiating structure and consideration.

The Initiating structure refers to the extent to which a leader is likely to define and structure his or her role and those of subordinates in the search for goal attainment. It includes behaviour that attempts to organize work, work relationships and goals. The leader characterized as high in the initiating structure could be described in terms such as, 'assigns group members to particular tasks'; 'expects workers to maintain definite standards of performance'; 'and emphasizes the meeting of deadlines'.

The Consideration is described as the existent to which a person is likely to have job relationships that are characterized by mutual trust, respect for subordinates' ideas, and regard for their feelings. He shows concern for his follower's comfort, well-being, status and satisfaction. A leader high in consideration could be described as one who helps subordinates with personal problems, being friendly and approachable and treats all subordinates as equals.

Consideration and mltlatmg structures were found to be uncorrelated and independent dimensions. They are separate behavioral categories and give rise to four types of leadership behaviour. Leaders may be

— Low on consideration and low on structure;

— Low on consideration and high on structure;

— High on consideration and high on structure; or

— High on consideration and low on structure.

Leadership behaviour could, therefore, be shown on two separate axes instead of along a single continuum. As a result four quadrants were developed which illustrated the different combinations of 'consideration' and 'structure'.

Extensive research based on these definitions, found that leaders high in initiating structure and consideration tended to achieve high subordinate performance and satisfaction more frequently than those who rated low on either consideration, initiating structure or both. The Ohio State studies suggested that the 'high-high' style generally resulted in positive outcomes, but enough exceptions were found to indicate that situational factors needed to be integrated into the theory.

MICHIGAN STUDIES

Leadership studies undertaken at the university of Michigan's Survey Research Center, at about the same time as those being done at Ohio State, had similar research objectives: to locate behavioural characteristics of leaders that appeared to be related to measure of performance effectiveness. Effective supervisors (measured along dimensions of group morale, productivity and cost reduction) appeared to display four common characteristics:

1. delegation of authority and avoidance of close supervision;
2. interest and concern in their subordinates as individuals;
3. participative problem-solving; and
4. high standards of performance.

The Michigan group came up with two dimensions of leadership behaviour which they labelled 'employee-oriented' and 'production-oriented'[85]. Leaders who were employee-oriented were described as emphasising interpersonal relationships; they took personal interest in the needs of their subordinates and accepted individual differences among members. The production-oriented leaders, in contrast, tended to emphasizing the technical or task aspects of the job keeping their main concern over accomplishing their group's task through the means of group members.

The conclusions arrived at by the Michigan researchers strongly favoured the leaders who were employee-oriented in their behaviour. Employee-oriented leaders were associated with high group productivity and higher job satisfaction. Production-oriented leaders tended to be associated with low group productivity and lower worker satisfaction.

LIKERT SYSTEM 4 MANAGEMENT

Rensis Likert[86], again incorporating the basic style categories of task orientation and employee orientation, devised a four-level model of management effectiveness.

In System 1 managers make all the work-related decisions and order their subordinates to carry them out. Standards and methods of performance are also rigidly set by them. Failure to meet the managers' goals results in threats or punishment. The managers feel little trust or confidence in their subordinates, and the subordinates, in turn, fear the managers and feel that they have little in common with them.

In System 2 managers still issue orders, but their subordinates have some freedom to comment on those orders. The subordinates are also given some flexibility to carry out their tasks but within carefully prescribed limits and procedures. Those subordinates who meet or exceed the manager's goals may be rewarded. In general, the managers have a condescending attitude towards their subordinates, and the subordinates are cautious when dealing with their managers.

In System 3, managers set the goals and issue general orders after discussing them with their subordinates. The subordinates can make their own decisions about how to carry out their task, since only broad and major decisions are made by high-level managers. Rewards, rather than the threats of punishment, are used to motivate the subordinates. The subordinates feel free to discuss most work-related matters with their managers, who, in turn, feel that to a larger extent the subordinates can be trusted to carry out their tasks properly.

System 4 is Likert's ideal system towards which organizations should work.

Goals are set and work-related decisions are made by the group. If managers formally reach a decision, they do so after incorporating the suggestions and opinions of the other group members. Thus, the goal they set or the decision they reach may not always be the one they personally favour. To motivate the subordinates, managers not only use economic rewards but also try to give their subordinates the feeling of worth and importance. Performance standards exist to permit self-appraisal by subordinates, rather than to provide the managers with a tool to control them. Interaction between the managers and subordinates is frank, friendly and trusting.

MANAGERIAL GRID

The managerial grid identifies a range of management behaviours based on the various ways that task-oriented and employee-oriented styles (each expressed as a continuum on a scale of 1 to 9) can interact with each other[87]. Thus, style 1, 1 management is an impoverished management with low concern for people and low concern for tasks or production. This style is some times called laissez-faire management, because the leader abdicates his or her leadership role.

Style 1,9 management is country club management in which there is high concern for employees but low concern for production. Style 9,1 management is task or authoritarian management with high concern for production and efficiency but low concern for employees. Style 5,5 is middle-of-the-road management in which there is an intermediate amount of concern for both production and employee satisfaction.

Style 9,9 management is team or democratic management in which is found a high concern for both production and employee morale and satisfaction. Blake and Mouton argue strongly that the 9,9 management style is the most effective type of leadership behaviour. This approach will, in almost all situations, result in improved performance, low absenteeism and turnover, and high employee satisfaction.

LEADERSHIP CONTINUUM

Another important work on leadership styles is that of Tannenbaum and Schmidt[88]. They suggest a continuum of possible leadership behaviour available to a manager and along which various styles of leadership may be placed. At one extreme of the continuum is the boss-centred leadership (authoritarian) and at the other extreme is the subordinate-centred leadership (democratic).

The continuum presents a range of action related to the degree of authority used by the manager and to the area of freedom available to the subordinates in arriving at decisions. Moving along the continuum, the manager may be characterised according to the degree of control that is maintained over the subordinates. Neither extreme of the continuum is absolute as there is always some limitation on authority and on freedom. This approach can be seen as identifying four main styles of leadership by the manager: tells, sells, consults, and joins.

Tells – the manager identifies the problem, chooses a decision and announces this to his subordinates, expecting them to implement it without an opportunity for participation.

Sells – the manager still chooses a decision but recognises the possibility of some resistance from those faced with the decision and attempts to persuade his subordinates to accept it.

Consults – the manager identifies the problem but does not choose a decision until the problem is presented to the group, and the manager has listened to the advice and solutions suggested by the subordinates.

Joins – the manager defines the problem and the limits within which the decision must be chosen and then passes on to the group, with the manager as a member, the right to make decisions.

Tannenbaum and Schmidt suggested that there are three factors or forces, of particular importance in deciding what types of leadership are practicable and desirable. These are: forces in the manager; forces in the subordinates; forces in the situation

Forces in the Manager: The manager's behaviour is influenced by his own personality, background, knowledge and experiences. These internal forces will include: value systems; confidence in subordinates; leadership inclinations; and feelings of security in an uncertain situation.

Forces in the Subordinates: The subordinates are influenced by many personality variables and their individual set of expectations about relationship with the manager. Characteristics of the subordinates are: the strength of the needs for independence; the readiness to assume responsibility for decision making; the degree of tolerance for ambiguity; interest in the problem and the feelings as to its importance; understanding and identification with the goals of an organization; necessary knowledge and experience to deal with the problem; and the extent of learning to expect to share in decision making.

Forces in the Situation: The manager's behaviour will be influenced by the general situation and environmental pressures. Characteristics in the situation include: type of organization; group effectiveness; nature of the problem; and pressure of time.

Tannenbaum and Schmidt[89] conclude that successful leaders are keenly aware of those factors or forces which are most relevant to their behaviour at a particular time. Successful managers are both perceptive and flexible.

Further, more attention would be given to the interdependency of the forces in the manager, in the subordinates and in the situation.

CONTINGENCY APPROACH TO LEADERSHIP

The disillusionment with the 'great man', trait and behavioural approaches to understanding leadership has turned the attention to the study of situations and the belief that leaders are the product of given situations. The contingency approaches to leadership attempt

1. to identify which of these factors is most important under a given set of circumstances; and

2. to predict the leadership style that will be most effective under those circumstances.

In this process several theories like Fiedler's Contingency Model, Vroom and Yetton Contingency Model, Path Goal Model, Life Cycle Theory, Tri-Dimensional Model and Learning Model have been advanced though, all of them woven around the theme of ' No Best Way'.

FIEDLER'S CONTINGENCY MODEL

One of the first leader-situation models was developed by Fiedler[90] In his Contingency theory of leadership effectiveness.

Fiedler suggested that leadership behaviour is dependent upon the favourability of the leadership situation. There are three major variables which determine the favourability of the situation and which affect the leader's role and influence.

Leader-Member Relations- The degree to which the leader is trusted and liked by the group members, and their willingness to follow the leader's guidance.

The Task Structure- the degree to which the task is clearly defined for the group and the extent to which it can be carried out by detailed instructions.

Position Power- the power of the leader by virtue of his position in the organization, and the degree to which the leader can exercise authority to influence. For ex: Rewards and punishments or promotion and demotions.

From these three variables, Fiedler constructed eight combinations of group-task situations through which to relate leadership style. When the situation is very favourable (good leader-member relations, structured task, strong position power) or very unfavourable (poor leader-member relations, unstructured task, weak position power), then a task-oriented leader (low Least Preferred Co-worker-LPC) with a directive controlling style will be more effective. When the situation is moderately favourable and the variables are mixed, then the leader with an interpersonal relationship orientation (high LPC) and a participative approach will be more effective.

Fiedler's Contingency model was based on studies of a wide range of group situations, and concentrated on the relationship between leadership and organizational performance. In order to measure the attitudes of the leader, Fiedler developed a 'least preferred co-worker' (LPC) scale. This measures the rating given by leaders about the person with whom they could work the least well. The questionnaire contained 20 items. Each item was given a single ranking between one to eight points, with eight points indicating the most favourable rating. For example

Pleasant 8 7 6 5 4 3 2 1 Unpleasant

The LPC score is the sum of the numerical ratings on all the items for the 'least preferred co-worker'. The less critical the rating of the least preferred co-worker and the more favourably evaluated, the higher the leader's LPC score.

Fiedler's work has been subjected to much criticism[91] but it does provide a further dimension to the study of leadership. The best style of leadership will be dependent upon the variable factors in the leadership situation. Fielder argues that leadership effectiveness may be improved by changing the leadership situation. Position power, task structure, leader-member relations can be changed to make the situation more compatible with the characteristics of the leaders.

VROOM AND YETTON CONTINGENCY MODEL

Vroom and Yetton[92] base their analysis on two aspects of a leader's decision: its quality and its acceptance.

Decision quality, or rationality, is the effect that the decision has on group performance. Decision acceptance refers to the motivation and commitment of group members in implementing the decision. A third consideration is:

The amount of time required to make the decision. This model suggests five main management decision styles.

Autocratic

A 1. The Leader solves the problem or makes the decisions alone Using information available at the time:

A II. The Leader obtains information from the subordinates but then decides on solution alone.

C 1. The problem is shared with the relevant subordinates, individually. The leader then makes the decision which mayor may not reflect the influence of subordinates.

C II. The problem is shared with subordinates as a group. The leader then makes the decision which mayor may not reflect the influence of subordinates.

Group

G 1. The problem is shared with subordinates as a group. The leader acts as chairperson, rather than an advocate. Together the leader and subordinates generate and evaluate alternatives and attempt to reach group consensus on a solution.

Vroom and Yetton suggest seven decision rules to help the manager discover the most appropriate leadership style in a given situation. The first three rules protect the quality of decisions and the last four the acceptance of decisions. These rules indicate decision styles that a manager should avoid in a given situation and indicate the use of others. Decision tree charts are introduced to help in the application of the rules and to relate the situation to the appropriate leadership style.

PATH-GOAL MODEL

The Path-goal theory of leadership, espoused by House[93], and House and Dessler[94] together is based on the belief that the individual's motivation is dependent upon the expectations that increased effort to achieve an improved level of performance will be successful, and the expectations that improved performance will be instrumental in obtaining positive rewards and avoiding negative outcomes.

It suggests that the performance of subordinates is affected by the extent to which the manager satisfies their expectations. The Path-goal theory hold that subordinates will see leadership behaviour as a motivating influence to the extent that it satisfies their expectations. Satisfaction of their needs is dependent upon effective performance; and the necessary direction, guidance, training and support, which would otherwise be lacking, are provided.

House identified four main types of leadership behaviour.

Directive leadership involves letting the subordinates know exactly what is expected of them and giving specific directions to them. The subordinates are expected to follow rules and regulations.

Supportive leadership involves a friendly and approachable manner, displaying concern for the needs and welfare of the subordinates.

Participative leadership involves consulting the subordinates and the evaluation of their opinions and suggestions before the manager makes the decision.

Achievement-oriented leadership involves setting challenging goals for the subordinates, seeking improvement in their performance and showing confidence in their ability to perform well.

This theory suggests that the different types of behaviour can be practised by the same person at different times in varying situations.

Leadership behaviour is determined by two main situational factors: the personal characteristics of subordinates and the nature of the task.

— The personal characteristics of subordinates determine how they will react to the manager's behaviour and the extent to which they see such behaviour as an immediate or potential source of need satisfaction;

— The nature of the task to the extent that it is routine and structured, or non-routine and unstructured.

Effective leadership behaviour is based, therefore, on both the willingness of the manager to help his subordinates and the needs of the subordinates for help. Leader behaviour will be motivational to the extent that it provides the necessary direction, guidance and support, helps clarify path-goal relationships and removes any obstacles, which hinder the attainment of goals. By using one of the four styles of leadership behaviour the manager attempts to influence' subordinates' perceptions and motivation, and smooth out the path to their goals.

LIFE-CYCLE THEORY OF LEADERSHIP

Paul Hersey and Kenneth H. Blanchard[95] have developed a situational theory of leadership. They call it the "Life-Cycle theory". This theory is based on the belief that the most effective leadership style varies with the maturity of followers. Maturity is viewed as consisting of two components, job-related maturity and psychological maturity. Job-related maturity refers to the ability to perform a task. Psychological maturity refers to a person's willingness to perform ajob.

Hersey and Blanchard considered task and relationship behaviour as either high or low and then combined them into four specific leadership styles: telling, selling, participating and delegating. They are described as follows:

1. *Telling* (high task-low relationship): The leader defines roles and tells people what, how, when and where to do various tasks. It emphasizes directive behaviour.
2. *Selling* (high task-high relationship): behaviour and supportive behaviour.
3. *Participating* (low task-high relationship): The leader and the follower share in decision-making, with the maih role of the leader being facilitating and communicating.
4. *Delegating* (low task-low relationship): The leader provides little direction or support.

Four distinct levels of maturity are:

RI Person is unwilling and unable to perform the job.

R2 Person is unable but willing to perform the job.

R3 Person is able but unwilling to perform the job.

R4 Person is able and willing to perform the job.

The life-cycle theory suggests that as the individual matures, the leadership style will change. When an employee is first brought into an organization, he is considered immature (Rl). Therefore, a high task-low relationship style of leadership (telling) is most appropriate to make the employee learn the new job. After he has learned the job, a high task-high relationship style (selling) is most appropriate (R2).

In the third phase, the employee has now matured (R3) to the point of seeking responsibility and taking the initiative to do the job. The leader should provide emotional support, but must not over direct and initiate structure in terms of task completion (participating style).

Finally, as the follower becomes confident, experienced, and self-motivated, the leader can practice a low task-low relationship style (delegating). A fully matured person (R4) expects to be able to operate with minimum influence from the leader. This can be considered a situation in which the follower's maturity and self-direction area substitute for leadership[96]. A person with a high level of skill, experience and self-motivation does not need a leader to structure the job.

REFERENCES

1. V.H Vroom, "Work and Motivation", Wiley Eastern, New Delhi, 1978, p. 6.
2. Berelson and Steinner, Bernard Berelson and Gray A. Steiner, "Human Behaviour", Harcourt, Brace and world, New york 1964.
3. William G.Scott, 'Organisation Theory', Homewood, III: Richard D. Irwin, 1977, p. 75
4. Daltan E.McFarland, "Management Principles and Practices" Newyork: Macmillian, 1974, p. 537.
5. R.M. Steers and L.W. Porter, "Motivation and Work Behaviour" Mc Graw Hill, New York, 1975 p. 5.
6. Pinder, C. "Work Motivation", Scott , Foresman and Co, Glenview III, 1984.
7. J.L Gray and F.A Starke, "Organisational Behaviour-Concepts and Applicatons", Merrill publishing Co., Columbus, 1988, p. 104.
8. Fred Luthans, "Organisational Behaviour", McGrawHill, New York, 1989, p. 231.
9. Lee. J.E.A. "The Gold and the Garbage in Management Theories and Prescriptions", Athens, Ohio University Press, pp. 7-11, 1980.
10. Handy, Charles B. "Understanding Organisation" Harmondsworth, Penguin Books Ltd., pp. 7-9, 1981.

11. A.H. Maslow, "A Theory of Human Motivation", Psychological Review, Vol. 50, 1943, pp. 370-396.
12. Maslow, A.H. "Motivation and Personality", New York, Harper and Row, 1970, Revision, pp. 21-23, 1970.
13. Herzberg. F.et. al: "The Motivation to Work", New York, John Wiely & Sons, pp. 7-17-1959.
14. Brayfield A.H. and Crocket W.H. "Employee Attitudes and Employee Performance", Psychological Bulletien LII pp. 127-139, 1955.
15. Dunnette, M.D. Campbell, J.P and Hackel, M.D. "Factors contributing to Job Satisfaction and Job Dissatisfaction in Six Occupational Groups, Organisational Behaviour and Human Performance", vol.2, pp. 143-174, 1967.
17. David C. McClelland," The Achievement Motive," New York: Apple, on Century–Crafts, 1953.
18. David C. MsClelland and Winter. D.G. "Motivating Economic Achievement", New York, The Free Press, pp. 127–129, 1969.
19. Lee. J.E.A. op.cit., pp. 19-21.
20. Atkinson. J.W. et.al "Motivation and Achievement", New York, John-Wiely & Sons, pp. 49-53, 1974.
22. Kanter P.S. "Power Failure in Management Circuits", Harvard Business Review, July-August, pp. 197-207, 1979.
23. Peters T.J. "Leadership: Sad facts and Silver linings", Harvard Business Review, November-December, pp. 217-238, 1979.
24. Menzies, H.D.: "The Ten Toughest Bosses"; Fortune, April 21, pp. 147-159, 1980.
25. Victor H. Vroom, 'Work and Motivation', New York, John Wiley, 1964. p. 69.
26. Vroom V.H. and Deci. E.L (Ed) "anagement & Motivation" Harmonds worth, Penguin Books Ltd. pp. 11-17, 1970.
27. Heneman, H.G and Schwab, D.B. "Evaluation of Research on Expectancy Theory: Predictors of employee performance", Psychological Bulletin, LXXVIII, pp. 147-163, 1972.
28. Robins, S.P pp. 224-225.
29. J. Stacy Adams, "Toward an understanding of Inequity", Journal of Abnormal and Social Psychology, Vol.67 (1963) pp. 422-436.

30. Richard A. Cosier and Dan R. Dalton, "Equity theory and Time: a Reformation", Academy of Management Review (April 1983), pp. 311-319.

31. Dunham, R.D., "Organisational Behaviour", Richard D. Irwin, Illinois, 1984, pp. 110-112.

32. L.W. Porter and E.E. Lawler, "Managerial Attitude and Performance", Homewood, III: Richard D. Irwin, 1968

33. Lawler, E.E. op.cit., pp. 14-19.

34. Georgopoulos, B.S. et.al, "A Path-Goal Approach to Productivity", Journal of Applied Psychology vol.41, 1957.

35. Handy, Charles. B. op.cit., pp. 17-21.

36. Douglas McGregor, "The Human Side of Enterprise", (New york: McGraw-Hill, 1960.)

37. Robins, S.P., Organisational Behaviour; Concepts and Contraversies; cit, p.209

38. B.F. Skinner, Beyond Freedom and Dignity (New York; Knopf, 1971). Also See–Fred Luthans and Robert Kreitner, "Orgnaisational Behaviour Modification and Beyond : An Operant and Social Leaving Approach" (Glenview, III.:Scott, Foresman and Company, 1984)

39. For an extensive discussion of the benefits of behaviour modification see, W. Clay Hamner and Ellen P.Hamner "Behaviour Modification on bottom Line", in J. Richard Hackman et.al., Perspective on Behaviour (1983) pp. 310-324.

40. Locke E., and Latham G. "Goal Setting : A Motivational Technique That Works", Prentice Hall, Englewood - Cliffs, N.J. 1984.

41. I. Bennis, W. G. "Leadership Theory and Administrative Behaviour: The Problem of Authority," *Administrative Science Quarterly,* VolA, 1959, pp. 259-269.

42. Gore, W.J. and Silander, F.S. "A Bibliographical Essay on Decision Making," *Administrative Science Quarterly,* Vo1.6, 1959, pp.121-129.

43. Stogdill, R.M., *Hand Book of Leadership: A Survey of Theory and Research,* Free Press, New York, 1974, p.7.

44. Kannel, B. "Leadership: A Challenge to Traditional Research Methods and Assumptions," *Academy of Management Review,* Vol.3, 1978, pp.475-482.

45. Peter Drucker, Practice of Management, Allied Publishers, New Delhi, 1970, p. 159.
46. Munson, C.E. "Style and Structure in Supervision", *Journal of Education for Social Work, 17*, 1981 pp.65-72.
47. Bennis, W.G. "Leadership Theory and Administrative Behaviour: The Problem of Authority," *Administrative Science Quarterly*, 4, 1959.
48. Hollander, E.P., and Jullian J.W., "Contemporary Trends in the Analysis of Leadership Processes," *Psychological Bulletin*, 71, 1996, pp. 387-391.
49. Fiedler, F.E., *A Theory of Leadership Effectiveness, McGraw Hill*, New York, 1967.
50. Merton, R.K. "The Social Nature of Leadership," *American Journal of Nursing*, 69, 1969, pp.2614-2618.
51. Bass, B.M., *Leadership and Performance Beyond Expectations*, The Free Press, New York, 1985.
52. Tichy, N.M. and Devanna, M.A., *The Transformational Leader*, Wiley, New York, 1986.
53. Roach, C.F. and Behling, O. "Functionalism: Basis for an Alternative Approach to the Study of Leadership," in *Leadership and Managers* by J.G. Hunt (ed.), Pergamon, New York, 1984.
54. Campbell, D.P. Campbell Leadership Index Manual, National Compute System, 1991.
55. Ginnett, R.C. "Team Effectiveness Leadership Model: Identifying Leverage Points for Change," Proceedings of the National Leadership Institute Conference, College Park, MD: National Leadership Institute, 1996.
56. Kakabadse, Andrew, "Leadership for the Third Millennium," *Essence of Leadership*, International Thompson Publishing, 1998.
57. Fiedler, F.E. "Style or Circumstance: The Leadership Enigma", *Psychology Today*, March, 1969, p.39
58. Vroom, V.H., *The Search for a Theory of Leadership in Contemporary Management: Issues and View Points*, Ed. Joseph W. McGuire, Englewood Cliffs, N.J., Prentice-Hall, 1974, p.396.
59. Ordway Tead, *The Art of Leadership*, McGraw Hill Book Company, Inc. New York, 1953, p.83.
60. Chester I. Barnard, *The Functions of the Executive*, Harvard University Press, Cambridge, 1946, p.260.

61. Henry Fayol, General and Industrial Management, Pitman and Sons, London, 1949.

62. George R. Terry, *Principles of Management*, Richard D. Irwin, Inc. Home Wood, Illinois, 1968, ppA61-463.

63. Ralph M. Stogdill, "Personal Factors Associated with Leadership: A Survey of the Literature", *Journal of Psychology*, Jan.1948, pp.35-71.

64. Keith Davis, *Human Behaviour at work*, 4th edition, Mc Graw Hill, New Delhi, 1972, pp.1 02-104.

65. Chris Argyris, Executive Leadership, Harper and Brothers Publishers, New York, 1953, pp. 4-5.

66. Harold Koontz and Heinz Weihrich, *Essentials of Management*, 5th Edition, McGraw Hill Series in Management, New York, 1990, p.345. .

67. Robert L. Katz, "The Skills of an Effective Administrator," *Harvard Business Review*, September-October 1974, pp.90-1 02.

68. Yuki, Gary., *Leadership in Organizations*, Prentice Hall, Englewood Cliffs, New Jersey, 1981.

69. Michael J. Marquart and Dean W. Engel, "HRD Competencies for a Shrinking World," *Training and Development*, May 1993, pp.62-64.

70. *Ibid.*, p.63.

71. Rabindra M. Kanungo and Sasi Misra, "Managerial Resourcefulness: A Reconceptualization of Management Skills," *Human Relations*, December 1992, pp.1311-1332.

72. David A. Whetten and Kim S. Cameron, *Developing Management Skills*, Harper Collins, New York, 1991, p.8.

73. *Ibid.*, p.11.

74. Gibb, C.A. "Leadership" in *Hand Book of Social Psychology* Edited by Lindzey, G. and Aronson, VolA, Addison-Wesley, Mass, 1969, pp.215-229.

75. Byrd, C. Social Psycholody, Appleton-Century-Crofts, 1940, pp. 183-188.

76. Jennings, E.E. "The Anatomy of Leadership", *Management of Personnel Quarterly*, Vol.l, Autumn, 1961, p.2.

77. Gheselli, E.E. "Management Talent", American Psychologist, Vol. 18, Oct, 1963, pp.631-642.

78. Stogdill, R.M. "Personal Factors Associated with Leadership: A Survey of Literature", *Journal of Psychology,* Vo1.25, 1948, ppJ 5-71.

79. Koontz, H. and O' Donnel, C., Management, McGraw-Hill, New York, 1976, p.591.

80. James Owen, "The Uses of Leadership Theory", *Michigan Business Review,* Vo1.25, No.1, January, 1973,pp.13-19.

81. McGregor, D. The Human Side of Enterprise, McGraw-Hill, New York, 1960, pp. 33-57.

82. Ouchi, W.G., *Theory Z: How American Business can meet the Japanese Challenge,* Addison-Wesley, 1981. p.4

83. Lewin, K., Lippitt, R. and White, R.K. "Patterns of Aggressive Behaviour in Experimentally Created 'Social Climates''', *Journal of Social Psychology,* Vol. 1 0, 1939, pp.271-299.

84. Steven Kerr, Chester, A. Schniesheim, Charles J. Murphy, and Ralph. M. Stogdill. "Toward a Contingency Theory of Leadership based upon the Consideration and Initiating Structure Literature", *Organizational Behaviour and Human Performance,* August 1974, pp.62-82.

85. Khan, R. and Katz D. "Leadership Practices in Relation to Productivity and Morale" in *Group Dynamics, Research and Theory,* 2nd Ed. D. Cartwright and A. Zander Elonsford, Row, Paterson, New York, 1960, pp.93-98.

86. Rensis Likert, New Pattern of Management, McGraw-Hill, New York, 1961, pp. 5-25.

87. Robert R. Blake and Jane S. Mouton., *The Managerial Grid,* (Gulf Publishing, Houston, 1978) Kurt Lewin, Ronald Lippitt and Ralph K. White "Patterns of Aggressive Behaviour in Experimentally Created Social Climates", *Journal of Social Psychology,* Vol.I0, No.2, May, 1939, pp.271-299.

88. Tannenbaum, R. and Schmidt, W.H. "How to Choose a Leadership Pattern," *Harvard Business Review,* May-June, 1973. pp.162-175, 17-8-180.

89. *Ibid.,* Retrospective Commentary, pp. 166-168.

90. Fiedler, F.E., *A Theory of Leadership Effectiveness,* McGraw-Hili, New York, 1967, pp.43-54.

91. Filley, A.C., House, RJ. and Kerr, S., *Managerial Process and Organizational Behaviour,* 2nd Ed. Scott, Foresman, 1976, p.223.

92. Vroom V.H. and Yetton P.W., *Leadership and Decision Making*, University of Pittsburgh Press, 1973, pp.64-69.

93. House RJ. "A Path-Goal Theory of Leadership Effectiveness", *Administrative Science Quarterly*, Vo1.16, Sep.I971, pp.321-338.

94. House RJ. and Dessler G. "The Path-Goal Theory of Leadership", in Hunt J.G. and Larson, L. (Eds) *Contingency Approaches to Leadership*, Souther Illionois, University Press, 1974, pp.43- 52.

95. Paul Hersey and Kenneth H. Blanchard, *Management of Organisational Behaviour*, Engle Wood Cliffs, Prentice Hall, New Jersey, 1979.

96. Steven Kerr and John M. Jermier, "Substitutes for Leadership: Their Meaning and Measurement", *Organisational Behaviour and Human Performance*, December 1978, pp.375-403.

2

RESEARCH DESIGN AND METHODOLOGY

STATEMENT OF THE PROBLEM

Motivation and leadership are the crucial issues in all organizations as every manager has to deal with these aspects in order to succeed in the organizational mission. Organizational researchers have been studying the topic of Motivation and leadership for many years. However, the motivation and leadership are closely interlinked with each other. As such a manager must be a good leader in order to motivate people to perform better in their jobs to achieve individual as well as organizational goals. Though the concepts of leadership and motivation are two sides of the same coin, they mean different things to different people.

No universal meaning can be associated with the motivation concept for a number of reasons. The concept of motivation or its derivatives, can be used as a noun, adjective, or adverb. Motivation is the cause of leadership and leadership is the effect of motivation. In the first stage it is the motive which influences the leader and in the second stage the leader influence the followers. Thus, they are multidimensional, multi-faceted, multi situational and multi role concepts.

The study of the subject of leadership is as old as civilization itself. Since past to the present many behavioural scientists, psychologists and management experts have tried to analyses, speak and write about the attitudes, characteristics and dynamics that go with leadership. The problem of leadership has been one of the man's major concerns since the days of antiquity. Leadership, similar to motivation, has been conveying many meanings to many people. Leader tries to motivate others in specific direction with the help of his traits like intelligence. As the specific findings of one research in a particular area and in a particular organization may not be totally relevant to other organizations, the research on these issues continue for ever.

What are the factors that effect motivation and leadership? What is the role of leader in motivating people? How to reconcile the motivation and leadership ? The present empirical book addresses these issues.

RELEVANCE OF THE STUDY

The establishment of Life Insurance Corporation of India in the year 1956 helped the Indian economy by developing saving habits in the people. The LIC has developed not only the saving habits but also made the people to protect their lives against the risk. As a government organisation, it has contributed and continuous to be the main source to the government revenue. Hence it is playing vital role in the Indian economy.

The nationalization of 14 commercial banks, in 1969 also occupy a vital place in the Indian economy with the increasing emphasis laid on the socialistic pattern of society by providing a new orientation to the Indian banking industry. These nationalized banks have strengthened the rural economy by expanding their banking facilities to the rural areas.

LIC and commercial banks come under service industry and their main aim is to render good service irrespective of 'The way they operate'. The performance of any organization depends upon its members i.e., employees. Motivation and effective leadership play very important role to improve the performance of employee which in turn improves the performance of the organisation.

In the present day era of liberalization, privatization and globalisation, the LIC and commercial banks have to compete with domestic and foreign agencies for providing good service and 'developing the right goods and service to the right people in right time'. It is possible with the improved performance, commitment and team work of their employees. Hence, it is the right time to make an attempt to study the motivation and leadership of the LIC and commercial bank employees.

The present micro level study is an attempt to investigate into the motivation and leadership of employees in LIC and CBB.

REVIEW OF LITERATURE

Some of the studies made by different authors in both theoretical and empirical spheres on motivation and leadership are presented in the following paragraphs.

MOTIVATION

Frederick W. Taylor's[1] Major work was published in 1911. His work was eventually led to improved recognition and productivity for industrial workers. The changes he brought to management paved the way for later development of organizational behaviour. To be sure, the goal was still technical deficiency, but at least management was awakened to the importance of one of its neglected resources. In 1920 Whiting Williams[2] was also published a significant interpretation of his experiences, What's on the Worker's Mind.

Elton Mayo and F.J. Roethlisberger[3] in his work gave academic stature to the study of human behaviour at work. They applied keen insight, straight thinking and sociological backgrounds to industrial experiments at the Western Electric Company. The result was the concept that an organization is a social system and the worker is in deed the most important element in it. Their experiments showed that the worker is not a simple tool but a complex personality interacting in a group situation that often is difficult to understand.

Herzberg[4] study on Maslow's model covered over 200 industrial accountants and engineers in Pittsburgh area. It reported that employees named different types of conditions for good and bad feelings. His study revealed that the factors responsible for job satisfaction are quite different from the factors that led to dissatisfaction, so identified were classified by his as 1. Motivational factors and 2. Hygiene or maintenance factors. Hygiene or maintenance factors are the context factors. According to him, they can dissatisfy by their absence but they can not satisfy by their presence.

One of McClellands[5] studies examined the motivational patterns that were emphasized in schools, books and families in different nations. His studies revealed that people's motivational patterns tended to agree with the cultural environment in which they grew up. He also found that nations with more achievement–motivated people tend to have faster social and economic development that leads to higher goals and drives, so the people do better work. They are not strongly 'money hungry', although they may acquire wealth in their drives to achieve. They work because of their desire for challenge, accomplishment, and service to others. It is estimated that 10 per cent of the people in the united states are highly achievement motivated[6].

Rao[7] has studied on the managers, supervisors and the workers of small industries perceive the organizational climate of these industries. There were no consistent differences in the perceptions of the managers, supervisors and workers and the differences shown were dependent on the units. The personal factors such as age, education, professional training and previous experience were not associated with their perceptions.

McClelland's[8] another study of power motivation reported that power-motivated people make excellent managers, if their drives are for institutional power instead of personal power. Institutional power is the need to influence others' behavior for the good of the whole organization. In other words, these people seek power through regular leadership channels, so they are accepted by others and rise to leadership because of their successful performance. However, if a person's drives are toward personal power and political manipulation, that person tends to be an unsuccessful organizational leader.

Stinson and Johnson's[9] study covered over 400 industrial workers and supervisors. It reported that both achievers and affiliators disliked structured tasks and wanted more job autonomy. The achievement oriented workers disliked the structured tasks because their jobs had less challenge and opportunity for decisions.

The reasons given by the affiliation-oriented workers were some what different. They disliked a structured task because it restricted their freedom to make contacts with friends and mix socially on the job.

E. Lawler and Suttle[10] made a research and found a little evidence to support Maslow's theory that human needs from hierarchy. They did note, however, that there were two levels of needs–biological and other needs–and that the other needs would emerge only when biological needs were reasonably satisfied. They found, further, that at the higher level, the strength of the needs varied with the individual; in some individuals social needs pre dominated, while in others self–actualization needs were strongest.

Rajappa has highlighted the importance of working environment in the analysis of work motivations. Results of his study reveals that organisations with achievement oriented climate were highly productive organisations.

Bansal[12] reported that qualities need for successful job performance of managers are job knowledge, decision making, good human relation, coordination, leadership, co-operations, communication, need for power, need for occupational achievement and intelligence.

Sharma[13] has also emphasized the importance of organizational climate in employee work motivation. Based on a survey of fifty industrial organizations in India, he observed that grievance handling, recognition and appreciation, participative management and scope for advancement are important factors in an organizational climate enhancing work motivation of the employees. In other words, what required is the improvement of quality of work environment and not merely the material benefits.

Edwin Locke (1968)[14] and a group of researchers have produced an impressive amount of support for the proportion that the setting of "specific hard but attainable goals" is related

to much higher levels of performance than is the setting of diffuse, easy or moderate goals such as "Do your best". He has shown that even individuals trying for a goal so high they rarely reach it perform better than those who are attempting to attain easy goals. A person's goal of performance will, according to loke, help a manager to predict the person's future performance and satisfaction. He argues that all other theories of motivation, such as expectancy theory, are insufficient unless they include a goal–setting dimension.

LEADERSHIP

Some of the studies made by different authors in both theoretical and empirical spheres are presented hereunder.

A series of pioneering leadership studies were conducted on high school children in the late 1930s by Ronald Lippitt and Ralph K. White[15] under the direction of Kurt Lewin at the University of Iowa. They studied the decision-making component of the leader's behaviour and classified leaders into three types as authoritarian, democratic and laissez-faire. One definite finding was the boys' over-whelming preference for the democratic leader. In individual interviews, nineteen of the twenty boys stated they like the democratic leader better than the authoritarian leader. The boys also chose the laissez-faire leader over the autocratic one in seven out of ten cases.

Leadership studies undertaken at the University of Michigan's Survey Research Centre[16] divide leadership into employee–Centered and production-centered. The conclusions arrived at by the Michigan researchers strongly favoured the leaders who were employee-oriented in their behaviour. Employee-oriented leaders were associated with higher group productivity and higher job satisfaction. Production-oriented leader tended to be associated with low group productivity and lower work satisfaction.

Krech and Crutchfield[17] (1948) proposed a number of leadership functions. These are executive, planner, policy maker, 'expert' external group representative, controller of internal relationships, purveyor of rewards and punishments, arbitrator and mediator, exemplar, symbol of the group, surrogate for individual responsibility, ideologist, father figure and scapegoat.

Hemphill[18] (1949) and his associates at Ohio State Leadership Studies developed a list of approximately 1,800 items describing different aspects of leader behaviour. The items were sorted by the research team into nine different categories or hypothetical subscale, with most items assigned to several subscales. However, 150 items were found on which sorters were agreed to subscale for assigning an item. These items were used to develop the first form of the Leader Behaviour Description Questionnaire (LBDQ)

Robert Tannenbaum and Warren H.Schmidt[19] (1958) see leadership as involving a high variety of styles, ranging from one that is highly boss-centered to one that is highly subordinate–centered. The styles vary with the degree of freedom a leader or manager grants to subordinates. They recognize the following styles:

1. Leader makes decision and announces it.
2. Leader makes decision and persuades subordinates to accept it.
3. Leader presents ideas and invites questions.
4. Leader presents tentative decision subject to change.
5. Leader presents problems, gets ideas and suggestions before making decisions.
6. Leader defines problems and limits of action and asks group to make decisions.
7. Leader permits group to function within limits defined by situations.

The theory recognizes which style of the leader is appropriate depends on the leaders, the followers and the situation and also concludes that the successful leader is one who can assess the forces and behave appropriately at any given time.

Sanderson and Nafe[20] (1929) have proposed four types of leaders: the static, the executive, the professional and the group leaders.

Pigors[21] (1936) has observed that leaders in-group work tend to act either as master or educator.

Levine[22] (1949) has identified four types of leaders. The charismatic leader helps the group rally around a common aim, but tends to become dogmatically rigid. The organizational leader highlights and tends to drive people to effective action. The intellectual leader usually lacks skill in attracting people. The informal leader tends to adopt his style of performance to group needs.

Ganguli[23] (1964) has conducted a study in a state owned engineering company on leadership behaviour. He reported that 46.9 percent of the managers and 31.0 percent of workers of a factory preferred autocratic organizational climate while only 12.30 percent of the managers preferred democratic climate. The existing environment was perceived to be autocratic by 51 percent of the managers and 43.6 percent of the workers.

Apple White[24] (1965) had summarized much of the research on leadership roles and functions, the question of why people attempt to lead, leadership under stress conditions, the relationship of communication to leadership, the problem of leader assessment and the concept of leadership styles.

Stogdill[25] (1965) found in 27 organizations that leader structure is related to follower satisfaction with organization, while consideration is associated with satisfaction with freedom of action.

Thiagarajan and Deep[26] (1970) found that authoritarian leaders as more influential than the persuasive, and the persuasive more than participative.

Evans[27] (1970) tested the path-goal hypothesis in two organizations. It was found that consideration and structure do not interact in path-goal facilitation but, rather, both consideration and structure acted separately to enhance path-goal instrumentality.

Fleishman and Simmons[28] (1970) studied the effectiveness of Israeli foremen. Those high in both consideration and structure were most effective. Those low on both scales were least effective.

Sadler[29] (1970) drew a comparison among the various leadership styles preferred by employees in British companies. This involved 1,270 men and.319 women employed by two companies engaged in the marketing of office and computer equipment and in research and development for computer facilities. Employees' preferences were recorded in terms of four leadership styles: 'Tells, Sells, Consults, Joins (i.e. four points in continuum beginning with authoritarian to democratic style). It was found that most employees preferred a 'consults' style (moderate participation) to other styles. However, the highest degree of satisfaction was associated with getting the style of leadership that employees wanted, regardless of the actual style.

The study of 120 managers by Jaggi[30] (1978) concludes that prevailing leadership styles appear to be between 'benevolent autocracy' and 'consultative' type. The study further indicates that the leadership style is associated with various factors such as age of the executives, their positions and functions and the size of the organizations. Thus, younger managers and managers in bigger sized companies are less authoritarian whereas the managers in production and technical areas are more authoritarian.

Singh[31] (1979) has studied 100 managers of Public Sector Enterprises and concluded that 3 per cent of managers adapted democratic style, 7 per cent autocratic style, 23 percent compromiser style, 31 percent bureaucratic style and 21 percent developer style. He has found that there is procedural rigidity in Public Sector Enterprises.

Kalra[32] (1980) has studied the pattern of styles of 70 managers and has found that most of the managers have their leadership behaviour guided by the situations in their organizations.

Sinha[33] (1980) in his study lists out three types of leadership styles as 1.Participative. 2. Authoritarian and 3. Nurturant-task leadership.

Habibullah and Sinha[34] (1980) studied five hundred and twenty-three executives of the Bharath Heavy Electrical Limited to find out various factors of leader behaviour. The responses of the executives to the leadership styles scales were factor analyzed by the principal component method and varimax rotation was used. Resultantly, they found the following ten usable factors: subordinate based participation; leader centered nurturance; authoritarianism; guidance and encouragement; direction; task-orientation; friendly-orientation; power; role performance, distance and discipline.

R.P. Singh and Janak Pandey[35] (1986) conducted a study to show pattern of relationship between three leadership styles (participative, authoritarian and authoritative) with different strategies of control, need–satisfaction and commitment with the organization. The study was conducted on a sample of 250 respondents comprising 150 workers, 50 supervisors and 50 line–managers of electronic equipment manufacturing large public undertaking in India. The study suggests that participative style leads to greater need–satisfaction and organizational commitment, and authoritative style is closer to participative leadership but it does not lead to commitment. The study also brings out that participative and authoritative are positive styles of leadership. Authoritative may substitute participative till conditions in an organization do not permit but participative style of leadership would not work till there is change in the socio-cultural milieu of the Indian Organizations.

Ansari[36] (1986) observes that NT (Nurturant-Task) is a forerunner of a 'participative' style in the reciprocal influence process between leaders and subordinates.

Neelam Varma[37] (1986) has made an attempt to examine the relative validity of the implicit leadership by testing two groups experienced (executives) and inexperienced (students) in an oil refinery. The study suggests that a leader's behaviour may be conceived of as a joint effect of all the five dimensions of leadership, i.e., Authoritarian style, Bureaucratic style, Nurturant, Participative and Task-orientation.

Hingar[38] (1986), in her study found that leadership styles do not exert much influence on job satisfaction. She also found that there is no difference in the leadership styles across managerial hierarchy and there is no difference in the judgement made by leader himself and by his subordinates.

In a study by Omer Bin Sayeed[39] (1990) attempted to examine conflict handling strategies, leadership behaviour and leadership styles (relationship and task-motivated styles) in a common framework. The study was conducted on 79 middle level managers who were undergoing various training programmes conducted at National Institute for Training in Industrial Engineering, Bombay, India. It was found that conflict management strategies represented two main conflict management styles, viz., Reciprocal Problem Solving Style and Authoritative System Supported Style, which tended to relate selectively with five leadership dimensions. Reciprocal conflict management style significantly related with Participative, Nurturant, and Task-oriented leadership behavior, while Authoritative Conflict Management Style had significant relationships with authoritarian and bureaucratic leadership behavior. The low esteem for coworker (task-motivated leadership style) had a strong relationship with the application of force as a conflict management strategy, besides revealing some moderating influences of esteem for coworker between leadership behavior and conflict management strategies.

Rama J. Joshi[40] (1991) explores the concept of managerial effectiveness as perceived by the Chief Executives. Based on interviews with the Chief Executives of units (covered by the study), certain dimensions of managerial effectiveness were identified. They are:

Leadership, inspiring, dynamic, motivating, gets respect of others, result oriented, desire to achieve, direct resources towards maximizing results,

Ability with people, good human relations skill, concern for people, identification with the company and its goals.

Understanding and discharging their own role in the organization, effective handling of problems/situations,

Innovative/doing something on their own initiative/ creative

Rajinder Kaur[41] (1993) has designed a study to investigate the psychological characteristics of democratic and autocratic managers as well as to find out the relationship between managerial styles and managerial success. 325 managers from

Bharat Electronics Limited, Banaglore comprised the sample. The study indicates that managerial success is not associated with managerial styles. A tendency towards the autocratic style prevails among the Indian managers. The psychological correlates reveal a qualitative difference in the characteristics of the democratic and the autocratic managers.

N. Panchanatham and others[42] (1993) attempted to explore the leadership and problem solving styles of executives of public sector organizations. The results indicate that the executives dominantly used democratic, authoritative and coaching styles of leadership, there were no significant relationships between leadership styles and problem solving styles and in the field of specialization of executives did not have any influence on their problem solving styles. The study suggested that the organization should design separate training programmes on problem solving and leadership styles and the executives of different branches should be considered equally for developmental programmes.

Manisha Agarwal and G.C.Agarwals'[43] (1995) study examined the relationship between junior and middle manager's power styles and their influence over different dimensions of decision-making activities through participativeness in three industrial organizations. Data analysis reveals the importance of the integrated power style in predicting managerial participativeness in goal–setting and conflict-handling. Findings have significant implications for reducing middle level managers' feelings of powerlessness by increasing the degree of their participation in activities affecting personal or organizational level outcomes with the utilization of an integrative approach to power exercise at the work place. The study also indicates the importance of monetary incentives for middle and junior managers for securing their effective participation in the decision–making activities.

S.Subramanian and K.Sajjan Raos'[44] (1997) study is an attempt to investigate the attitudes of union leaders towards certain management decisions. Data have been gathered from 68 union leaders belonging to two prominent unions. Their perceived importance of the 12 crucial management activities and also their perceived contribution of the unions (as opposed to management) in implementing these aspects have been studied. Results reveal a positive orientation of union leaders towards these aspects and suggest that unions have metamorphosed from their traditional role of just getting their colleagues their due, to a more progressive outlook. The authors envisage a more dynamic functioning for union leaders in the changing realities by which they can contribute not only to the welfare of their colleagues, but also towards development of their organization.

V. Ravichandran and D.Nagabrahmam's[45] (1997) study attempted to explore the effectiveness of leadership in a transitory environment. A list of 15 traits/skills such as vision, expertise, motivation, calculated-risk, innovativeness, exemplary, assertion, integrity, charisma, interpersonal skills, initiativeness, ambition, altruism, commitment and empathy were identified through interaction process based on which a questionnaire was constructed and rated on five-point Likert scale. Data were collected from 299 managers representing 8 nationalized banks and their branches. The study states that effective leadership was perceived to be related to the person and his character such as one's expertise with interpersonal capabilities and empathy. The study also suggests that effective leaders are those with vision and having noble and altruistic goals. It is also noted that the ideal of leadership in everybody's mind has influencing effect on leadership in organizations if it is properly communicated and shared among top echelons.

Syed Vazith Hussain[46] (2002) made an attempt to analyse different leadership styles in small scale industries at micro level. The decision making styles are identified by him are: Style I Benevolent autocrat; Style II Strict autocrat; Style III Prior consultation; Style IV Democratic style and Style V Delegation. He collected data from 98 owner-managers of small scale industries. He concluded that owner-managers in small scale industries are adopting different styles depending upon the situation even though they are free from adopting any style. The results of the study strongly confirms the view that leadership is situational and effective leader should be flexible enough to adopt to the differences among the subordinates and situations.

OBJECTIVES OF THE STUDY

The specific objectives of the study are:

1. To study the perspectives of motivation of employees in L.I.C. and Commercial Bank Branches in association with the socio economic and organization position variables;
2. To examine the relationship of Leadership styles with certain socio economic and organization position variables of employees between L.I.C. and Commercial Bank Branches;
3. To find out the differences in Leadership styles as perceived by leader and subordinates between L.I.C. and Commercial Bank Braches; and
4. To examine the impact of Leadership on motivation of employees in LIC and Commercial Bank Branches.

HYPOTHESES

The hypotheses formulated for the study are the following :

1. There is no significant difference between LIC and commercial bank employees in motivation.
2. There is no significant difference between employees of LIC in motivation.
3. There is no significant difference between employees of commercial bank branches in motivation.
4. There is no significant difference between LIC and CBB employees under high degree of motivation.
5. There is no significant difference between LIC and CBB employees under their low degree of motivation.
6. There is no significant difference between LIC and CBB employees under their moderate degree of motivation.
7. There is no significant inter relationship among socieconomic and organizational position variables (henceforth SEOP) of employees of LIC.

8. There is no significant inter relationship among SEOP variables of employees of CBB.
9. There is no significant relationship between SEOP variables and leadership styles of employees of LIC.
10. There is no significant relationship between SEOP variables and leadership styles of employees of CBB.
11. There is no significant relationship among leadership styles of employees of LIC.
12. There is no significant relationship among leadership styles of employees of CBB.
13. There is no significant difference among different leadership styles in the inter levels of employees of LIC in self perception about their styles.
14. There is no significant difference among different leadership styles in the inter levels of employees of LIC as perceived by their subordinates.
15. There is no significant difference in leadership styles of employees of LIC as judged by leader himself and as judged by his subordinates.
16. There is no significant difference among different leadership styles in the inter levels of employees of CBB in self perception about their styles.
17. There is no significant difference among different leadership styles in the inter levels of employees of CBB as perceived by their subordinates.
18. There is no significant difference in leadership styles of employees of CBB as judged by leader himself and as judged by his subordinates.
19. There is no significant difference among different leadership styles of employees of LIC and CBB in self perception about their styles.
20. The is no significant difference among different leadership styles of employees of LIC and CBB as perceived by their subordinates.
21. There is no significant difference between LIC and CBB employees in impact of leadership on motivation.
22. There is significant difference between employees of LIC in impact of leadership on motivation.

23. There is no significant difference between employees of CBB in impact of leadership on motivation.
24. There is no significant difference between LIC and CBB employees under High Degree of impact of leadership on motivation.
25. There is no significant difference between LIC and CBB employees under Low Degree of impact of leadership on motivation.
26. There is no significant difference between LIC and CBB employees under Moderate Degree of impact of leadership on motivation.

AREA OF THE STUDY

The study covers the region, Nellore District of Andhra Pradesh, India (L 13.30" and 15.51" and 70.5 and 80.61") which is spread over an area of 13160 Sq. Km. The district head quarters, Nellore is the major town the Revenue divisions of Kavali, Nellore, Gudur and sub divided into 15 blocks and 46 mandals for administrative and micro–management of developmental activities. The district is at present constituted into 3 municipalities and 1201 villages.

The District has a population of 26.60 lakhs as per 2001 census constituting 3.68 percent of total population of Andhra Pradesh. It has rural population of 20.56 lakhs constituting 77 percent of the total district population. Out of the total population male and female population constitutes 13.41 lakhs and 13.18 lakhs respectively. 40.6 percent of the population in the district are literates. The average density of population is 202 per Sq. km.

Altogether at the time of the present study, there are 40 branches of Syndicate Bank which are acting as Lead bank in the district, 27 branches of State Bank of India, 27 branches of Andhra Bank and 46 branches of other nationalised banks.

(Distribution of the Commercial banks is presented in Table 1)

The LIC operating in Nellore District since 1956 with 8 branches. (Distribution of LIC Branches is presented in Table 2.)

Table 1
Distribution of Commercial Banks in Nellore District

Name of the Bank	*Number of Branches*
Syndicate Bank	40
State Bank of India	27
Andhra Bank	30
Other Nationalized Banks*	46
Total	143

Source : Lead Bank Office. Annual action plans, Nellore District.
* Other Banks includes Corporation Bank, Canara Bank, Bank of Borada, State Bank of Hyderabad, Indian Bank and Punjab National Bank etc.

Table 2
Distribution of LIC Branches in Nellore District

Name of the Branches	*Number of branches*
Nellore (Divisional Office)	1
Nellore (Branches)	3
Naidupet	1
Gudur	1
Atmakur	1
Kavali	1
Total	8

Source: Information collected from LIC Divisional office, Nellore.

Distribution of personnel employed in banks and LIC in Nellore District is Presented in Table 3.

The total number of personnel employed in the Commercial banks in the district are 1523 consisting of 91 Higher Level Executives, 104 Middle Level Executives, 326 Lower Level Executives and 1002 clerical staff and in LIC there are 486 personnel consisting of 15 Higher Level Executives, 79 Middle Level Executives, 64 Lower Level Executives and 328 clerical staff.

Table 3
Distribution of Personnel Employed in CBB and LIC

Organisation	*Higher Level Executives*	*Middle Level Executives*	*Lower Level Executives*	*Clerical Staff*	*Total*
Banks	91	104	326	1002	1523
IC	15	79	64	328	486

Methodology

The study is mainly based on primary data collected from a sample chosen for this purpose from the employees of LIC and CBB in Nellore District by making personal visits through a schedule prepared for this purpose. The primary data are collected in three phases. In the first phase the purpose and objectives of the schedule are explained to them and requested them to go through the schedule thoroughly. In the second phase doubts with any of the respondents about the contents of the schedule are clarified. In the third phase the data are collected through schedules from the respondents.

SAMPLING

The present study confines to superiors and subordinates, hierarchical levels in L.I.C. and Commercial Bank employees with a view to find out the differences between them. Stratified Random Sampling Technique with proportional allocation method have been used.

The Sample number of employees drawn from each cadre in L.I.C. is given below:

Table 4
L.I.C

Designation	*Total Number of Employees*	*Sample drawn*
Divisional manager, Marketing Manager, Managers, D.T.C., Principal. (Higher Level Executives)	15	9
Branch Managers, Assistant Branch Managers, Administrative Officers, (Middle Level Executives)	79	49
Assist Administrative Officers, Supervisors, Development officers. (Lower level Executives)	64	40
Higher grade Assistants, Lower grade Assistants, Record Clerks/Typists.	328	202
Total	486	300

The sample number of employees drawn from each cadre in Commercial Banks is given below.

Table 5
Commercial Banks

Designation	*Total Number of Employees*	*Sample drawn*
Asst. General Manager, Sr. Manager IV, Chief Manager, Divisional Managers. (Higher Level Executives)	91	30
Lead District Manager, Manager, Sub Managers, Deputy Managers. (Middle Level Executives)	104	34
Jr. Managers, Asst. Managers, Probationary Officer, Field Officers, Accountants (Lower level Executives)	326	107
Computer Operators, Spl. Cashiers, Cashiers, Sr. Assistants, Spl. Assistants clerks, Typists.	1002	329
Total	1523	500

TOOLS FOR DATA COLLECTION

In the present study, five schedules were used for the data collection.

Schedule–I (Personal profile) is designed to elicit the information relating to SEOP Variables viz, age, designation, experience, education qualification and economic status.

Schedule–II is designed to know the opinion on some factors relating to motivation. This schedule consists of 40 items.

Schedule–III is designed to know the opinion on some factors relating to leader's self-perception. It consists of 30 items. It was administered to Higher Level Executives, Middle Level Executives, Lower Level Executives with a view to judge their own leadership styles. This schedule measures five leadership styles viz., Authoritarian (A), Participative (P), Bureaucratic (B), Task-orientation(T) and Nurturant (N) each of these categories consists of six items.

Schedule–IV is used to measure leader's behaviour as perceived by his subordinates (subordinates perception on superior styles). This schedule consists of 30 items measuring the above five leadership styles, each of those categories consists of six items.

Schedule–V is used to measure the impact of leadership on motivation of subordinate. This schedule consists of 40 items.

Tools for Analysis

The data collected through the schedules from primary sources have been processed and the results are tested with the hypotheses by employing appropriate statistical tools like *mean, standard deviation and 't' values,* etc.

1. The Chief managers, divisional managers, A.G. Managers, D.T.C. principal and Marketing manager are treated as peers at the Higher Level Executives.
2. The branch managers, A.O.s. senior managers, deputy managers, lead managers, assistant branch managers are at the Middle Level Executives.
3. The Junior managers, assistant managers, sub managers, probationary officers, special officers, development officers assistant administrate officers, development officers, accountants are treated as Lower Level Executives.
4. The Special grade assistants, senior assistants, clerks, special cashiers, cashiers, higher grade assistants, lower grade assistants clerks, typists are non executive subordinates or clerks.

The variables under taken for the study are viz. age, designation, experience, education and economic status.

The leadership styles were measured in two ways i.e., as judged by leader himself (leader's self perception) and as judged by his immediate subordinates' (subordinates' perception on superior style).

In L.I.C. the Divisional Manager, Marketing Manager, Managers, D.T.C., Principal. (Higher Level Executives). Branch Managers, Assistant Branch Managers, Administrative Officers, (Middle Level Executives), Assist Administrative Officers, Supervisors, Development officers. (Lower level Executives), Higher grade Assistants, Lower grade Assistants, Record clerks/Typists are taken at the lower level as clerks for the analysis of leadership styles.

In Commercial Banks, Asst. General Manager, Sr. Manager

IV, Chief Manager, Divisional Manager (Higher Level Executives). Lead District Manager, Manager, Sub-Managers, Deputy Managers (Middle Level Executives). Jr. Managers, Asst. Managers, Probationary Officer, Field Officers, Accountants (Lower Level Executives). Computer Operators, Spl. Cashiers, Cashiers, Sr. Assistants, Spl. Assistants, Clerks, Typists are taken at the lower level as clerks for the analysis of leadership styles.

Five leadership styles judged by leader himself and as judged by his subordinates' viz, authoritarian, participative, bureaucratic, task-orientation and Nurturant were taken for the study.

Scoring Pattern

The opinions of the employees are obtained with the help of five-point scaling technique. The scale descriptions of schedule II and V using. 1. SA – (Strongly Agree) 2. A – (Agree) 3. MA – (Moderately Agree) 4. D – (Disagree) 5. SD – (Strongly disagree)

And the scale descriptions of schedule III and IV using 1. Q.T. – (Quite True) 2. T – (True) 3. D– (Doubtful) 4. F – (False) 5. Q.F – (Quite False.)

For the purpose of quantification of the opinions expressed by the employees through the schedule the scale descriptions are quantified in the following manner.

Scale Descriptions		*Scores*
S A	Q T	5
A	T	4
M A	D	3
D A	F	2
SD A	Q F	1

There are six items of each style and the maximum score was 30 while minimum was 6.

Item No.3, 22, 23,26,27 and 28 represent Authoritarian style. Item No.1,6,7,10,19 and 29 represent Participative style. Item No.9,13, 17,20,24 and 25 represent Bureaucratic style. Item

No.5,8,11,14,18, and 21 represent Task – orientation style. Item No.2,4,12,15, 16, and 30 represent Nurturant style.

Field Study

The field investigation was conducted by adopting the personal interview method. During the investigation considerable help has been received from head office officials, managers, officers and clerical staff of the LIC and commercial banks are under the study in Nellore District, there were, however, problems in collecting the personal data as well as the perceptions about the leadership and motivation their experiences with superiors, peers and sub-ordinates due to the inhibition to express freely about the organisation and its members. These problems, of course, could be overcome by developing acquaintance with the respondents, approaching more number of times and visiting the bank and LIC branch offices.

Scope of the Study

The study is confined to the officers from Higher Level Executives, Middle Level Executives, Lower Level Executives and Non Executives or Clerical Staff in L.I.C. and Commercial bank branches. It examines the perspectives of the motivation of employees and the leadership styles as perceived by leader himself, subordinates' perception on their superior's leadership styles, and impact of leadership on motivation of subordinates. Though this is a micro study, the conclusions would be relevant to all organizations working in similar environment.

Limitations of the Study

The study used for the purpose of collecting the opinions of employees has the following limitations.

1. Certain behavioural and management terms used for purpose of research are new to the respondents, as they are not in general use.
2. Sub staff personnel have been excluded from the study as it is assumed that they lack comprehensive view to respond.

Therefore, in the process of data collection these limitations are handled by adopting appropriate measures like informal discussions and interviews so as to collect reliable and dependable information.

Chapter Design

The study is organized into Eight Chapters.

Chapter One	Reviews the introductory concepts, theories and approaches of motivation and leadership.
Chapter Two	Presents the statement of the problem, research methodology, review of literature and design of the study.
Chapter Three	Covers the perspectives of motivation of employees in L.I.C. and Commercial Bank Branches.
Chapter Four	Analyses the leaders' self perception on superiors styles.
Chapter Five	Analyses the subordinates' perceptions on superiors styles.
Chapter Six	Analyses the differences of leadership styles of L.I.C. and Commercial Bank Branches.
Chapter Seven	Incorporates the impact of leadership on motivation of subordinates.
Chapter Eight	Presents the summary of findings and conclusions.

REFERENCES

1 Frederick W.Taylor, "The Principles of Scientific Management", New York: Harper & Brothers, 1911.

2. Whiting Williams, "What's on the Workers Mind", New York : Charles Scribner's Sons, 1920.

3. Elton Mayo, 'The Human problems of an Industrial Civilization', Cambridge, Mass.; Harvard University Press, 1933; F.J.Roethlisberger and W.J.Dickson, "Management and the Worker", Cambridge, Mass : Harvard University Press, 1939..

4. Herzberg. F. et.al : 'The Motivation to work' New York John Wiely & Sons, 1959.

5. The original work on achievement motivation is David C.McClelland, "The Achieving Society", New York : D.Van Nostrand Company, 1961.
6. Fred Luthans, "Organizational Behaviour" 2d ed., New York : Mc Graw Hill Book Company, 1977, p.322.
7. Rao, T.V. "A study of the perception of the organizational climate by the Employees of Small Industries". Paper presented in 10th Annual Conference, Indian Academy of Applied Psychology, April, 1972.
8. David C.McClelland and David H.Burnham, "Power is the Great Motivator", Harvard Business Review, March-April, 1976, pp.100-110.
9. John E.Stinson and Thomas W.Johnson, "Tasks, Individual Differences and Job Satisfaction" Industrial Relations, October, 1977, pp.315-322.
10. E. Lawler III and J.L. Suttle, 'A Casual Correlation Test of the Need–Hierarchy Concept,' Organisational Behavious and Human Performance (April, 1972).
11. Rajappa, P.: 'Motivation Management,' National Labour Institute Bulletin, June, 1978.
12. Bansal, M.R. : 'Correlates of Managerial Effectiveness' Ph.D. Thesis IIT, Delhi-1982.
13. Sharma, B.R. : 'Employee Motivation and Employer - Employee Relations in India', Indian Management, June, 1983.
14. Locke. E., and Latham G, "Goal Setting; A Motivational Technic that Works", Prentice–Hall, Englewood–Clifts, N.J. 1984.
15. Lewin, Lippitt, R., and White, R.K. "Patterns of Aggressive Behaviour in Experimentally Created 'Social Climates'," Journal of Psychology, 1939, pp.271-299.
16. Daniel Katz et. al. "Productivity, Supervision and Morale in Office Situation," Survey Research Centre, University of Michigan, Ann Arbor, 1950.
17. Krech, E. and Crutchfield, R.S., Theory and Problems of Social Psychology, McGraw Hill, New York, 1948.
18. Hemphill, J.K. "The Leader and his Group," Journal of Educational Research, 28 (1949).
19. Robert Tannenbaum and Warren H. Schmidt "How to choose a Leadership Pattern," Harvard Business Review (March–April 1958), pp.95-101, and Heinz Weihrich, "How to Change a Leadership pattern," Management Review (April 1979) pp.26-28, 37-40.
20. Sanderson, D. and Nafe, R.W. "Studies in Rural Leadership," Publ. Amer. Social. Soc., 23 (1929), pp.163-175.
21. Pigors, P. "Types of Leaders in Group Work," Sociology and Social Research , 21 (1936), pp.3-17.
22. Levine, S. "An Approach to Constructive Leadership," Journal of Sociological Issues, 5 (1949), 46-53.
23. Ganguli, H.C., Structure and Process of Organisation, Asia Publishing House, Bombay, 1964.
24. Apple White, Phillip B., Organisational Behaviour, Engle Wood Cliffs, Prentice-Hall, New Jersey, 1965 (Chapter 6).

25. Stogdill, R.M. "Managers, Employees, Organisations," Bureau of Business Research, Ohio State University, Columbus, 1965.
26. Thiagarajan, K.M. and Deep, S.D. "A Study of Supervisor Subordinate Influence on Satisfaction in four Cultures," Journal of Social Psychology, 82 (1970), 173-180.
27. Evans, M.G. "The Effect of Supervisory Behaviour on the Path-Goal Relationship," Organizational Behaviour and Human Performance, 5 (1970), pp.277-297.
28. Fleishman, E.A. and Simmons, J. "Relationship between Leadership Patterns and Effectiveness ratings among Israeli foreman," Personnel Psychology, 23 (1970), pp.169-172.
29. Sadler, P.J. "Leadership Style, Confidence in Management, and Job Satisfaction," Journal of Applied Behavioural Science, 6 (1970), pp.3-19.
30. B.L. Jaggi, "Management Leadership Styles in Indian Work Organizations," Indian Manager, April-June 1978.
31. Singh, P. "Leadership Process and its Impact on Productivity, Satisfaction and Work Commitment," Decision, Volume 6, 1979, pp.259-269.
32. H.K. Kalra "Leadership Styles of Executives in Indian Enterprises," unpublished Research Report, Punjab Agricultural University, Ludhiana, 1980.
33. Sinha, J.B.P., The Nurturant Task-Behaviour, Concept Publishing Company, New Delhi, 1980.
34. Habibullah, A.H.M. and Sinha, J.B.P. "Motivational Climate and Leadership Styles," Vikalpa, 5 (1980).
35. R.P. Singh and Janak Pandey "Leadership Styles, Control Strategies and Personal Consequences," Indian Journal of Industrial Relations, Volume 22, No.1, July 1986, pp.41-51.
36. Ansari, M.A. "Need for Nurturant-Task Leaders in India: Some empirical evidence," Management and Labour Studies, 11,1, (1986), pp.26-36.
37. Neelam Varma, "A Test of Implicit Personality Theories of Leadership," Indian Journal of Industrial Relations, Volume 22, No.2, Oct, 1986, pp.189-198.
38. Hingar Asha, Leadership Styles and Job Satisfaction, Printwell Publishers, Jaipur, 1986.
39. Omer Bin Sayeed "Conflict Management Styles: Relationship with Leadership Styles and Moderating Effect of Esteem for Coworker," Indian Journal of Industrial Relations, Vol.26, No.1, July 1990, pp.28-52.
40. Rama J. Joshi "Managerial Effectiveness: As Perceived by Chief Executives," Indian Journal of Industrial Relations, Volume 27, No.1, July 1991, pp.69-78.
41. Rajinder Kaur "Managerial Styles in the Public Sector," Indian Journal of Industrial Relations, Volume 28, No.4, April, 1993, pp.363-367.
42. N. Panchanatham, K. Rajendran, and K. K. Karuppiah "A Study of Executive Leadership Styles and problem Solving Behaviour," Indian Journal of Industrial Relations, Volume-29, No.1, July 1993.
43. Manisha Agarwal and G.C. Agarwal "Relationship of Middle Managers' Power Styles with their Participativeness at the Work Place," Indian

Journal of Industrial Relations, Volume 30, No.3, January 1995, pp.278-288.

44. Subramanian and K. Sajjan Rao "Attitudes of Union Leaders in Changing Realities- Direction Towards Greater Involvement," Indian Journal of Industrial Relations, Volume 32, No.4, April 1997. pp.409-422.
45. V. Ravichandran and D. Nagabrahmam "Leadership in a Transitory Environment," Indian Journal of Industrial Relations, Volume 32, No.4, April 1997, pp.423-435.
46. Syed Vazith Hussain "Leadership Styles in Small Scale Industries," The Indian Journal of Commerce, Vol.55, No.3, July-September 2002, pp.45-54.

3

MOTIVATION IN INSURANCE AND BANKING SECTOR

INTRODUCTION

The efficiency and effectiveness of organizations depend on the motivation and it affects individuals and groups in the organizations from the view-point of their morale, discipline, attitudes, aptitudes, and other behavioural dimensions including inter-personal relationships. Therefore, the managers put forth their efforts to the best of their ability in motivating their employees at all levels so as to get the best out of them without much unsought consequences.

In order to know the difference of motivation among the employees of LIC and CBB the data is interpreted and presented in the following paragraphs:

The study pertain to know the following findings.

1. The difference between motivation of LIC and CBB employees;
2. The difference between motivation of LIC and CBB employees viz., Higher Level Executives, Middle Level Executives, Lower Level Executives and Clerks;
3. The difference between motivation of LIC and CBB at inter levels of employees viz., Higher Level Executives and Middle Level Executives, Middle Level Executives and Lower Level Executives, Lower Level Executives and Clerks; and

4. The difference between high, moderate and low degree of motivation of LIC and CBB employees.

MOTIVATION OF LIC AND CBB EMPLOYEE GRADES

The degree of motivation of employees among higher, middle, lower level executives and clerks is worked and the analysis and results are presented in the following tables.

Motivation of LIC and CBB Employees

Table 1, reveals that the LIC employees have shown higher motivation than the CBB employees as the mean score of LIC employees (155.663) is higher than the mean score of the CBB employees (145.968). As the calculated 't' value 7.585 is greater than the critical value, it is significant at 0.01 level. Hence, the hypothesis, that there is no significant difference between LIC and CBB employees in motivation is rejected.

Table 1
Motivation of LIC and CBB Employees

SECTOR	*N*	*Mean*	*S.D.*	*t' value*
LIC	300	155.663	18.456	7.585
CBB	500	145.968	15.783	

Source: Compiled from field survey

For 't' value, the degree of freedom (df) is N_1+N_2-2. In LIC, employees stood 300 where $N_1=300$, in CBB, employees stood 500, where $N_2=500$, the $df=N_1+N_2-2 \Rightarrow 300+500-2=798$. For 798 df the entries at 0.01 and 0.05 by linear interpolation are 2.576 and 1.960. The 't' values with two stars are significant at 0.01 level and those with one star at 0.05 level

Motivation of Higher Level Executives of LIC and CBB

Table 2, reveals that the LIC Higher Level Executives have shown higher motivation than the CBB Higher Level Executives as the mean score of LIC Higher Level Executives (167.556) is being higher than the mean score of the CBB Higher Level Executives (150.833). As the calculated 't' value 3.542 is greater than the critical value, it is significant at 0.01 level.

Hence, the hypothesis, that there is no significant difference between LIC and CBB employees in motivation is rejected.

Table 2
Motivation of LIC and CBB Higher Level Executives

SECTOR	*N*	*Mean*	*S.D.*	*t' value*
LIC	9	167.556	11.193	3.542
CBB	30	150.833	15.851	

Source: Compiled from field survey

For 't' value, the degree of freedom (df) is N_1+N_2-2. In LIC, Higher Level Executives stood 9 where $N_1=9$, in CBB, Higher Level Executives stood 30, where $N_2=30$, the $df=N_1+N_2-2=>9+30-2=37$. For 37 df the entries at 0.01 and 0.05 by linear interpolation are 2.042 and 2.750. The 't' values with two stars are significant at 0.01 level and those with one star at 0.05 level.

Motivation of Middle Level Executives of LIC and CBB

Table 3, reveals that the LIC Middle Level Executives have shown higher motivation than the CBB Middle Level Executives as the mean score of LIC Middle Level Executives (152.449) is being higher than the mean score of the CBB Middle Level Executives (141.912). As the calculated 't' value 3.374 is greater than the critical value, it is significant at 0.01 level. Hence, the hypothesis, that there is no significant difference between LIC and CBB employees in motivation is rejected.

Table 3
Motivation of LIC and CBB Middle Level Executives

SECTOR	*N*	*Mean*	*S.D.*	*t' value*
LIC	49	152.449	13.999	3.374
CBB	34	141.912	13.975	

Source: Compiled from field survey

For 't' value, the degree of freedom (df) is N_1+N_2-2. In LIC, Middle Level Executives stood 49 where $N_1=49$, in CBB, Middle Level Executives stood 34, where $N_2=34$, the $df=N_1+N_2-2=>49+34-2=81$. For 81 df the entries at 0.01 and 0.05 by linear interpolation are 2.660 and 2.000. The 't' values with two stars are significant at 0.01 level and those with one star at 0.05 level.

Motivation of Lower Level Executives of LIC and CBB

Table 4, reveals that the LIC Lower Level Executives have shown higher motivation than the CBB Lower Level Executives as the mean score of LIC Lower Level Executives (161.575) is being higher than the mean score of the CBB Lower Level Executives (153.159). As the calculated 't' value 0.032 is greater than the critical value, it is significant at 0.01 level. Hence, the hypothesis, that there is no significant difference between LIC and CBB employees in motivation is rejected.

Table 4

Motivation of LIC and CBB Lower Level Executives

SECTOR	*N*	*Mean*	*S.D.*	*t' value*
LIC	40	161.575	15.059	3.032
CBB	107	153.159	14.757	

Source: Compiled from field survey

For 't' value, the degree of freedom (df) is N_1+N_2-2. In LIC, Lower Level Executives stood 40 where N_1=40, in CBB, Lower Level Executives stood 107, where N_2=107, the df=N_1+N_2-2=>40+107-2=145. For 145 df the entries at 0.01 and 0.05 by linear interpolation are 2.576 and 1.960. The 't' values with two stars are significant at 0.01 level and those with one star at 0.05 level.

Motivation of Clerks of LIC and CBB

Table 5, reveals that the LIC Clerks have shown higher motivation than the CBB Clerks as the mean score of LIC Clerks (154.743) is being higher than the mean score of the CBB Clerks (143.605). As the calculated 't' value 6.8 is greater than the critical value, it is significant at 0.01 level. Hence, the hypothesis, that there is no significant difference between LIC and CBB employees in motivation is rejected.

For 't' value, the degree of freedom (df) is N_1+N_2-2. In LIC, Clerks stood 202 where N_1=202, in CBB, Clerks stood 329,

Table 5
Motivation of LIC and CBB Clerks

SECTOR	*N*	*Mean*	*S.D.*	*t' value*
LIC	202	154.743	19.856	6.8
CBB	329	143.605	15.504	

Source: Compiled from field survey

where N_2=329, the df=N_1+N_2-2=>202+329-2=529. For 529 df the entries at 0.01 and 0.05 by linear interpolation are 2.576 and 1.960. The 't' values with two stars are significant at 0.01 level and those with one star at 0.05 level.

Motivation of LIC Higher Level Executives and Middle Level Executives

Table 6, reveals that the LIC Higher Level Executives have shown higher motivation than the LIC Middle Level Executives as the mean score of LIC Higher Level Executives (167.556) is being higher than the mean score of the LIC Middle Level Executives (152.449). As the calculated 't' value is 3.569 greater than the critical value, it is significant at 0.01 level. Hence, the hypothesis,that there is no significant difference between employees of LIC in motivation is rejected.

Table 6
Motivation of LIC Higher Level Executives and Middle Level Executives

Job level	*N*	*Mean*	*S.D.*	*t' value*
Higher Level Executives	9	167.556	11.193	3.569
Middle Level Executives	49	152.449	13.999	

Source: Compiled from field survey

For 't' value, the degree of freedom (df) is N_1+N_2-2. In LIC, Higher Level Executives stood 9 where N_1=9, Middle Level Executives stood 49, where N_2=49, the df=N_1+N_2-2=>9+49-2=56. For 56 df the entries at 0.01 and 0.05 by linear interpolation are 2.704 and 2.021. The 't' values with two stars are significant at 0.01 level and those with one star at 0.05 level.

Motivation of LIC Middle Level Executives and Lower Level Executives

Table 7, reveals that the LIC Lower Level Executives have shown higher motivation than the LIC Middle Level Executives as the mean score of LIC Lower Level Executives (161.575) is being higher than the mean score of the LIC Middle Level Executives (152.449). As the calculated 't' value is 2.925 greater than the critical value, it is significant at 0.01 level. Hence, the hypothesis, that there is no significant difference between employees of LIC in motivation is rejected.

Table 7
Motivation of LIC Middle Level Executives and Lower Level Executives

Job level	*N*	*Mean*	*S.D.*	*t' value*
Middle Level Executives	49	152.449	13.999	2.925
Lower Level Executives	40	161.575	15.059	

Source: Compiled from field survey

For 't' value, the degree of freedom (df) is N_1+N_2-2. In LIC, Middle Level Executives stood 49 where $N_1=49$, Lower Level Executives stood 40, where $N_2=40$, the $df=N_1+N_2-2=>49+40-2=87$. For 87 df the entries at 0.01 and 0.05 by linear interpolation are 2.660 and 2.000. The 't' values with two stars are significant at 0.01 level and those with one star at 0.05 level.

Motivation of LIC Lower Level Executives and Clerks.

Table 8, reveals that the LIC Lower Level Executives have shown higher motivation than the LIC Clerks as the mean score of LIC Lower Level Executives (161.575) is being higher than the mean score of the LIC Clerks (154.743). As the calculated 't' value 2.475 is greater than the critical value, it is significant at 0.05 level. Hence, the hypothesis, that there is no significant difference between employees of LIC in motivation is rejected.

For 't' value, the degree of freedom (df) is N_1+N_2-2. In LIC, Lower Level Executives stood 40 where $N_1=40$, Clerks stood 202, where $N_2=202$, the $df=N_1+N_2-2=>40+202-2=240$. For 240 df the entries at 0.01 and 0.05 by linear interpolation are

Table 8
Motivation of LIC Lower Level Executives and Clerks

Job level	*N*	*Mean*	*S.D.*	*t' value*
Lower Level Executives	40	161.575	15.059	2.475
Clerks	202	154.743	19.856	

Source: Compiled from field survey

2.576 and 1.960. The 't' values with two stars are significant at 0.01 level and those with one star at 0.05 level.

Motivation of CBB Higher Level Executives and Middle Level Executives

Table 9, reveals that the CBB Higher Level Executives have shown higher motivation than the CBB Middle Level Executives as the mean score of CBB Higher Level Executives (150.833) is being higher than the mean score of the CBB Middle Level Executives (141.912). As the calculated 't' value 2.374 is greater than the critical value, it is significant at 0.05 level. Hence, the hypothesis, that there is no significant difference between employees of CBB in motivation is rejected.

Table 9
Motivation of CBB Higher Level Executives and Middle Level Executives

Job level	*N*	*Mean*	*S.D.*	*t' value*
Higher Level Executives	30	150.833	15.851	2.374
Middle Level Executives	34	141.912	13.975	

Source: Compiled from field survey

For 't' value, the degree of freedom (df) is N_1+N_2-2. In CBB, Higher Level Executives stood 30 where $N_1=30$, Middle Level Executives stood 34, where $N_2=34$, the $df=N_1+N_2-2 \Rightarrow 30+34-2=62$. For 62 df the entries at 0.01 and 0.05 by linear interpolation are 2.704 and 2.021. The 't' values with two stars are significant at 0.01 level and those with one star at 0.05 level.

Motivation of CBB Middle Level Executives and Lower Level Executives

Table 10, revels that the CBB Lower Level Executives have shown higher motivation than the CBB Middle Level

Executives as the mean score of CBB Lower Level Executives (153.159) is being higher than the mean score of the CBB Middle Level Executives (141.912). As the calculated 't' value 4.033 is less than the critical value, it is not significant at 0.05 level. Hence, the hypothesis, that there is no significant difference between employees of CBB in motivation is accepted.

Table 10

Motivation of CBB Middle Level Executives and Lower Level Executives

Job level	*N*	*Mean*	*S.D.*	*t' value*
Middle Level Executives	34	141.912	13.975	4.033
Lower Level Executives	107	153.159	14.757	

Source: Compiled from field survey

For 't' value, the degree of freedom (df) is N_1+N_2-2. In CBB, Middle Level Executives stood 34 where $N_1=34$, Lower Level Executives stood 107, where $N_2=107$, the df=N_1+N_2-2=>34 +107-2=139. For 139 df the entries at 0.01 and 0.05 by linear interpolation are 2.576 and 1.960. The 't' values with two stars are significant at 0.01 level and those with one star at 0.05 level.

Motivation of CBB Lower Level Executives and Clerks

Table 11, reveals that the CBB Lower Level Executives have shown higher motivation than the Clerks as the mean score of CBB Lower Level Executives (153.159) is being higher than the mean score of the Clerks (143.605). As the calculated 't' value 5.745 is greater than the critical value, it is significant at 0.01 level. Hence, the hypothesis, that there is no significant difference between employees of CBB in motivation is rejected.

Table 11

Motivation of CBB Lower Level Executives and Clerks

Job level	*N*	*Mean*	*S.D.*	*'t' value*
Lower Level Executives	107	153.159	14.757	5.745
Clerks	329	143.605	15.504	

Source: Compiled from field survey

For 't' value, the degree of freedom (df) is N_1+N_2-2. In CBB, Lower Level Executives stood 107where $N_1=107$, Clerks stood 329, where $N_2=329$, the $df=N_1+N_2-2=>107+329-2=434$. For 434 df the entries at 0.01 and 0.05 by linear interpolation are 2.576 and 1.960. The 't' values with two stars are significant at 0.01 level and those with one star at 0.05 level.

DEGREE OF MOTIVATION OF LIC AND CBB EMPLOYEES

The degree of motivation of employees is classified as high, moderate and low. The scores of the employees are arranged in descending order. The top 27 per cent of the sample employees is categorized as high and the bottom 27 per cent as low. The remaining employees come under the moderate category.

High Degree of Motivation of LIC and CBB Employees

Table 12, reveals that the LIC employees under High Degree of Motivation have shown higher motivation than the CBB employees under High Degree of Motivation as the mean score of LIC employees (174.086) is being higher than the mean score of the CBB employees (166.963). As the calculated 't' value 6.859 is greater than the critical value, it is significant at 0.01 level. Hence, the hypothesis, that there is no significant difference between LIC and CBB employees under their high degree of motivation is rejected.

Table 12

High Degree of Motivation of LIC and CBB Employees

Sector	*N*	*Mean*	*S.D.*	*t' value*
LIC	81	174.086	6.404	6.859
CBB	135	166.963	8.789	

Source: Compiled from field survey

For 't' value, the degree of freedom (df) is N_1+N_2-2. In LIC, High Degree of Motivation of LIC employees stood 81 where $N_1=81$, High Degree of Motivation of CBB employees stood 135, where $N_2=135$, the $df=N_1+N_2-2=>81+135-2=214$. For

214df the entries at 0.01 and 0.05 by linear interpolation are 2.576 and 1.960. The 't' values with two stars are significant at 0.01 level and those with one star at 0.05 level.

Low Degree of Motivation of LIC and CBB Employees

Table 13, reveals that the LIC employees under Low Degree of Motivation have shown higher motivation than the CBB employees under Low Degree of Motivation as the mean score of LIC employees (134.988) is being higher than the mean score of the CBB employees (128.148). As the calculated 't' value 2.984 is greater than the critical value, it is significant at 0.01 level. Hence, the hypothesis, that there is no significant difference between LIC and CBB employees under their low degree of motivation is rejected.

Table 13
Low Degree of Motivation of LIC and CBB Employees

Sector	*N*	*Mean*	*S.D.*	*t' value*
LIC	81	134.988	20.16	2.984
CBB	135	128.148	5.643	

Source: Compiled from field survey

For 't' value, the degree of freedom (df) is N_1+N_2-2. In LIC, Low Degree of Motivation of LIC employees stood 81 where $N_1=81$, Low Degree of Motivation of CBB employees stood 135, where $N_2=135$, the df=N_1+N_2-2=>81+135-2=214. For 214 df the entries at 0.01 and 0.05 by linear interpolation are 2.576 and 1.960. The 't' values with two stars are significant at 0.01 level and those with one star at 0.05 level.

Moderate Degree of Motivation of LIC and CBB Employees

Table 14, reveals that the LIC employees under Moderate Degree of Motivation have shown higher motivation than the CBB employees under Moderate Degree of Motivation as the mean score of LIC employees (156.986) is being higher than the mean score of the CBB employees (144.104). As the calculated 't' value 22.808 is greater than the critical value, it is significant at 0.01 level. Hence, the hypothesis, that there is no significant difference between LIC and CBB employees under their moderate degree of motivation is rejected.

Table 14
Moderate Degree of Motivation of LIC and CBB Employees

Sector	*N*	*Mean*	*S.D.*	*t' value*
LIC	138	156.986	5.193	22.808
CBB	230	144.104	5.332	

Source: Compiled from field survey

For 't' value, the degree of freedom (df) is N_1+N_2-2. In LIC, Moderate Degree of Motivation of LIC employees stood 138 where $N_1=138$, Moderate Degree of Motivation of CBB employees stood 230, where $N_2=230$, the $df=N_1+N_2-2 => 138+230-2=366$. For 366 df the entries at 0.01 and 0.05 by linear interpolation are 2.576 and 1.960. The 't' values with two stars are significant at 0.01 level and those with one star at 0.05 level.

4

LEADERSHIP STYLES IN INSURANCE AND BANKING SECTOR

INTRODUCTION

The behaviour of human beings much more in the capacity of leaders affects not only the behaviour and performance of others but also of the organizations. However, the behaviour of the leaders is closely related to the perceptions and attitudes they maintain concerning their purposes, roles and functions. The perceptions are consolidated from their self perceptions and their perceptions towards their own leaders who influenced or guided their missions and methods. Thus the performance of the leaders is the outcome of the approaches they adopt in their jobs which are the effects of their own perceptions about their own leaders. The nature of person, without any exception to a leader is to emulate and imitate their own ideal personalities. What are the perceptions of different employees in different grades in their leadership role relating to the inspiration and influence they have drawn from their predecessors. The analysis of the employees in several grades starting from Higher Level Executives down to Clerks forms the subject matter of this chapter.

The organisational efficiency depends on the leadership effectiveness. Leadership effectiveness varies with the socio-economic organizational position variables. Besides this, the styles like authoritarian, participative, bureaucratic, task-orientation and nurturant of the leaders influence the followers and their performance resulting in overall efficiency of the people and effectiveness of the organisation. The hierarchical positions of LIC and CBB included for the study cover Higher Level Executives, Middle Level Executives, Lower Level Executives and Clerks. The socio-economic organizational position variables include viz., designation, age, experience, education and economic status.

In LIC the sample of the study was 300 employees and in CBB the sample of the study was 500 employees belonging to four levels. Being at the extreme levels in the hierarchy the subordinates' perception has not been taken into account in the case of Higher Level Executives and the self perception is ignored in the case of Clerks, they being in the bottom of the hierarchy.

Thus, the leader's self perception reveals about the styles of Higher Level Executives, Middle Level Executives and Lower Level Executives of LIC and CBB. Scores on five leadership styles were computed from leader's evaluation of ones own style.

The correlations among selected socio-economic and organizational position variables were computed. Following this, the correlations of socio-economic and organizational position variables with leadership styles were computed. In addition, correlations were computed among five leadership styles.

In this chapter the presentation and discussion of the data pertain to the following:

I. Inter-correlation of SEOP variables of employees of LIC and CBB viz., Higher Level Executives, Middle Level Executives, Lower Level Executives and Clerks.

II. Relationship of SEOP variables with leadership styles of employees of LIC and CBB viz., Higher Level Executives, Middle Level Executives and Lower Level Executives.

III. Inter-correlation of leadership styles of employees of LIC and CBB viz., Higher Level Executives, Middle Level Executives and Lower Level Executives.

INTER-CORRELATION OF SEOP VARIABLES OF EMPLOYEES OF LIC

Higher Level Executives of LIC

Table 1 presents the inter-correlations among socio-economic and organizational position variables viz., designation, age, experience, education, and economic status for Higher Level Executives of LIC. The variable 'age' was significantly but negatively correlated with 'education' (r= -0.762, P<0.05) indicating that higher the age had lower the 'education'.

Table 1
Inter-correlations Among SEOP Variables for Higher Level Executives of LIC (N=9)

SEOP Variables	*Designation*	*Age*	*Experience*	*Education*	*Economic Status*
Designation		-0.607	-0.365	0.610	0.189
Age			0.556	*-0.762	-0.540
Experience				*-0.742	-0.368
Education					0.115
Economic Status					

Source: Compiled from field survey

The variable 'experience' was significantly but negatively correlated with 'education' (r= -0.742, P<0.05) indicating that higher the experience had lower the 'education'.

None of the other socio-economic and organizational position variables, however, were found not to be significantly inter-correlated. They are rather, independent of each other. Hence, the hypothesis, that there is no significant inter relationship among socio-economic and organizational position variables of employees of LIC is rejected in the case of age vs education and experience vs education, and is accepted in all other cases.

For the inter-correlation, the degree of freedom (df) is N-2. Higher Level Executives of LIC stood 9, where N=9, the df=9-2=7. For 7 df the entries at 0.01 and 0.05 by linear interpolation are 0.798 and 0.666 respectively (for 3 decimals). The correlation values with two stars are significant at 0.01 level and those with one star is significant at 0.05 level.

INTER-CORRELATION OF SEOP VARIABLES OF EMPLOYEES OF CBB

Higher Level Executives of CBB

Table 2 presents the inter-correlations among socio-economic and organizational position variables viz., designation, age, experience, education, and economic status for Higher Level Executives of CBB. The variable 'designation' was significantly but negatively correlated with 'experience' (r= -0.395, P<0.05) indicating that higher the 'designation' had lower the 'experience'.

Table 2
Inter-correlations Among SEOP Variables for Higher Level Executives of CBB (N=30)

SEOP Variables	*Designation*	*Age*	*Experience*	*Education*	*Economic Status*
Designation		0.052	*-0.395	0.186	-0.062
Age			*0.449	*0.369	-0.349
Experience				-0.178	-0.090
Education					0.333
Economic Status					

Source: Compiled from field survey

The variable 'age' was significantly and positively correlated with 'experience' (r= 0.449, P<0.05) indicating that higher the age greater the 'experience'. 'age' was also significantly and positively correlated with 'education' (r= 0.369, P<0.05) indicating that higher the 'education', higher the age.

None of the other socio-economic and organizational position variables, however, were found not to be significantly inter-correlated. They are rather, independent of each other. Hence, the hypothesis, that there is no significant inter relationship among socio-economic and organizational position variables of employees of CBB is rejected in the case of 'designation' vs experience, age vs experience and age vs education, and is accepted in all other cases.

For the inter-correlation, the degree of freedom (df) is N-2. Higher Level Executives of CBB stood 30, where N=30, the df=30-2=28. For 28 df the entries at 0.01 and 0.05 by linear interpolation are 0.463 and 0.361 respectively (for 3 decimals). The correlation values with two stars are significant at 0.01 level and those with one star is significant at 0.05 level.

Comparison of Higher Level Executives of LIC and CBB

In Higher Level Executives of LIC, 'designation' does not correlate significantly with any of the socio-economic and organisational position variables whereas in Higher Level Executives of CBB, 'designation' was significantly but negatively correlated with 'experience'. In Higher Level Executives of LIC, 'age' was significantly but negatively correlated with 'education' whereas in Higher Level Executives of CBB, 'age' was significantly and positively correlated with 'experience' and 'education'. In Higher Level Executives of LIC, 'experience' was significantly but negatively correlated with 'education' whereas in Higher Level Executives of CBB, 'experience' does not correlate significantly with any of the socio-economic and organisational position variables.

Middle Level Executives of LIC

Table 3 presents the inter-correlations among socio-economic and organizational position variables viz., designation, age, experience, education, and economic status for Middle Level Executives of LIC. The variable 'age' was significantly and positively correlated with 'experience'($r=0.327$, $P<0.05$) indicating that higher the age, greater the 'experience. 'age' was also significantly but negatively correlated with 'education' ($r= -868$, $P<0.01$) indicating that higher the age had lower the 'education'. 'age' was also significantly but negatively correlated with 'economic status' ($r= -322$, $P<0.01$) indicating that higher the age had lower the 'economic status'.

The variable 'experience' was significantly but negatively correlated with 'education' ($r= 0.318$, $P<0.05$) indicating that the persons who are at greater experience had lower education.

Table 3
Inter-correlations Among SEOP Variables for Middle Level Executives of LIC (N=49)

SEOP Variables	*Designation*	*Age*	*Experience*	*Education*	*Economic Status*
Designation		-0.204	-0.024	0.160	0.037
Age			*0.327	**-0.868	*-0.322
Experience				*-0.318	-0.277
Education					0.150
Economic Status					

Source: Compiled from field survey

None of the other socio-economic and organizational position variables, however, were found not to be significantly inter-correlated. They are rather, independent of each other. Hence, the hypothesis, that there is no significant inter relationship among socio-economic and organizational position variables of employees of LIC is rejected in the case of age vs experience, age vs education, age vs economic status and experience vs education, and is accepted in all other cases.

For the inter-correlation, the degree of freedom (df) is N-2. Middle Level Executives of LIC stood 49, where N=49, the df=49-2=47. For 47 df the entries at 0.01 and 0.05 by linear interpolation are 0.365 and 0.282 respectively (for 3 decimals). The correlation values with two stars are significant at 0.01 level and those with one star is significant at 0.05 level.

Middle Level Executives of CBB

Table 4 presents the inter-correlations among socio-economic and organizational position variables viz., designation, age, experience, education, and economic status for Middle Level Executives of CBB. The variable 'age' was significantly and positively correlated with 'experience' (r= 0.814, P<0.01) indicating that higher the age had greater the 'experience'.

None of the other socio-economic and organizational position variables, however, were found not to be significantly inter-correlated. They are rather, independent of each other. Hence, the hypothesis, that there is no significant inter relationship among socio-economic and organizational position variables of employees of CBB is rejected in the case of age vs experience, and is accepted in all other cases.

Table 4
Inter-correlations Among SEOP Variables for Middle Level Executives of CBB (N=34)

SEOP Variables	*Designation*	*Age*	*Experience*	*Education*	*Economic Status*
Designation		-0.045	-0.014	-0.174	0.017
Age			**0.814	-0.208	-0.038
Experience				-0.244	0.117
Education					0.299
Economic Status					

Source: Compiled from field survey

For the inter-correlation, the degree of freedom (df) is N-2. Middle Level Executives of CBB stood 34, where N=34, the df=34-2=32. For 32 df the entries at 0.01 and 0.05 by linear interpolation are 0.437 and 0.339 respectively (for 3 decimals). The correlation values with two stars are significant at 0.01 level and those with one star is significant at 0.05 level.

Comparison of Middle Level Executives of LIC and CBB

In Middle Level Executives of LIC and CBB, 'age' was significantly and positively correlated with 'experience'. In Middle Level Executives of LIC, 'age' was significantly but negatively correlated with 'education' and 'economic status' whereas in Middle Level Executives of CBB, 'experience' does not correlate significantly with 'education' and 'economic status'.

Lower Level Executives of LIC

Table 5 presents the inter-correlations among socio-economic and organizational position variables viz., designation, age, experience, education, and economic status for Lower Level Executives of LIC. The variable 'designation' was significantly and positively correlated with 'economic status'(r=0.465, P<0.01) indicating that higher the 'designation', greater the 'economic status'.

The variable 'age' was significantly and positively correlated with 'experience'(r=0.447, P<0.01) indicating that higher the age, greater the 'experience. 'Age' was also significantly but negatively correlated with 'education' (r=-0.373, P<0.05) indicating that higher the age had lower the 'education'.

Table 5
Inter-correlations Among SEOP Variables for Lower Level Executives of LIC (N=40)

SEOP Variables	*Designation*	*Age*	*Experience*	*Education*	*Economic Status*
Designation		-0.163	0.064	0.207	**0.465
Age			**0.447	*-0.373	0.311
Experience				-0.194	*0.423
Education					0.275
Economic Status					

Source: Compiled from field survey

The variable 'experience' was significantly and positively correlated with 'economic status' (r= 0.423, P<0.05) indicating that the persons who have greater experience had higher 'economic status'.

None of the other socio-economic and organizational position variables, however, were found not to be significantly inter-correlated. They are rather, independent of each other. Hence, the hypothesis, that there is no significant inter relationship among socio-economic and organizational position variables of employees of LIC is rejected in the case of designation vs economic status, age vs experience, age vs education, and experience vs economic status, and is accepted in all other cases.

For the inter-correlation, the degree of freedom (df) is N-2. Lower Level Executives of LIC stood 40, where N=40, the df=40-2=38. For 38 df the entries at 0.01 and 0.05 by linear interpolation are 0.434 and 0.315 respectively (for 3 decimals). The correlation values with two stars are significant at 0.01 level and those with one star is significant at 0.05 level.

Lower Level Executives of CBB

Table 6 presents the inter-correlations among socio-economic and organizational position variables viz., designation, age, experience, education, and economic status for Middle Level Executives of CBB. The variable 'age' was significantly, positively and highly correlated with 'experience' (r= 0.902, P<0.01) indicating that higher the 'age' had greater 'experience'.

Table 6
Inter-correlations Among SEOP Variables for Lower Level Executives of CBB (N=107)

SEOP Variables	*Designation*	*Age*	*Experience*	*Education*	*Economic Status*
Designation		-0.036	0.010	-0.049	0.016
Age			**0.902	0.057	-0.045
Experience				0.085	-0.074
Education					0.086
Economic Status					

Source: Compiled from field survey

None of the other socio-economic and organizational position variables, however, were found not to be significantly inter-correlated. They are rather, independent of each other. Hence, the hypothesis,that there is no significant inter relationship among socio-economic and organizational position variables of employees of CBB is rejected in the case of age vs experience, and is accepted in all other cases.

For the inter-correlation, the degree of freedom (df) is N-2. Lower Level Executives of CBB stood 107, where N=107, the df=107-2=105. For 105 df the entries at 0.01 and 0.05 by linear interpolation are 0.249 and 0.191 respectively (for 3 decimals). The correlation values with two stars are significant at 0.01 level and those with one star is significant at 0.05 level.

Comparison of Lower Level Executives of LIC and CBB:

In Lower Level Executives of LIC, 'designation' was significantly and positively correlated with 'economic status' whereas in Lower Level Executives of CBB 'designation' does not correlate significantly with any of the socio-economic and organisational position variables. In Lower Level Executives of LIC and CBB, 'age' was significantly and positively correlated with 'experience'. In Lower Level Executives of LIC, 'age' was significantly but negatively correlated with 'education' whereas in Lower Level Executives of CBB, 'age' does not correlate significantly with 'education' and 'economic status'. In Lower Level Executives of LIC, 'experience' was significantly but positively correlated with 'economic status' whereas in Lower Level Executives of CBB, 'experience' does not correlate significantly with any of the socio-economic and organisational position variables.

Clerks of LIC

Table 7 presents the inter-correlations among socio-economic and organizational position variables viz., designation, age, experience, education, and economic status for clerks of LIC. The variable 'age' was significantly and positively correlated with 'experience'(r=0.545, P<0.01) indicating that higher the age, greater the 'experience.

Table 7
Inter-correlations Among SEOP Variables for Clerks of LIC (N=202)

SEOP Variables	*Designation*	*Age*	*Experience*	*Education*	*Economic Status*
Designation		-0.020	-0.053	0.039	-0.012
Age			**0.545	-0.089	-0.048
Experience				**0.204	-0.101
Education					-0.007
Economic Status					

Source: Compiled from field survey

The variable 'experience' was significantly and positively correlated with 'education' (r= 0.204, P<0.05) indicating that the persons who have greater experience had higher 'education'.

None of the other socio-economic and organizational position variables, however, were found not to be significantly

inter-correlated. They are rather, independent of each other. Hence, the hypothesis, that there is no significant inter relationship among socio-economic and organizational position variables of employees of LIC is rejected in the case of age vs experience, and experience vs education, and is accepted in all other cases.

Clerks of CBB

Table 8 presents the inter-correlations among socio-economic and organizational position variables viz., designation, age, experience, education, and economic status for Middle Level Executives of CBB. The variable 'age' was significantly and positively correlated with 'experience' (r= 0.809, P<0.01) indicating that higher the age greater the 'experience'. 'Age' was also significantly and positively correlated with 'education' (r= 0.249, P<0.01) indicating that higher the age, higher the 'education'.

Table 8
Inter-correlations Among SEOP Variables for Clerks of CBB (N=329)

SEOP Variables	*Designation*	*Age*	*Experience*	*Education*	*Economic Status*
Designation		0.085	0.074	-0.030	0.012
Age			**0.809	**0.249	-0.101
Experience				**0.240	-0.034
Education					**-0.152
Economic Status					

Source: Compiled from field survey

The variable 'experience' was significantly and positively correlated with 'education' (r= 0.240, P<0.01) indicating that higher the 'experience', higher the 'education'.

The variable 'education' was significantly but negatively correlated with 'economic status' (r= -0.152, P<0.01) indicating that higher the 'education' had lower the 'economic status'.

None of the other socio-economic and organizational position variables, however, were found not to be significantly inter-correlated. They are rather, independent of each other.

Hence, the hypothesis, that there is no significant inter relationship among socio-economic and organizational position variables of employees of CBB is rejected in the case of age vs experience, age vs education, experience vs education and education vs economic status, and is accepted in all other cases.

For the inter-correlation, the degree of freedom (df) is N-2. clerks of CBB stood 329, where N=329, the df=329-2=327. For 327 df the entries at 0.01 and 0.05 by linear interpolation are 0.143 and 0.109 respectively (for 3 decimals). The correlation values with two stars are significant at 0.01 level and those with one star is significant at 0.05 level.

Comparison of Clerks of LIC and CBB

In Clerks of LIC and CBB, 'age' was significantly and positively correlated with 'experience' and also in clerks of CBB 'age' was significantly and positively correlated with 'education'. In Clerks of LIC and CBB, 'experience' was significantly and positively correlated with 'education'. In Clerks of LIC, 'education' does not correlate significantly with 'economic status' whereas in clerks of CBB, 'education' was significantly and positively correlated with 'economic status'.

RELATIONSHIP OF SEOP VARIABLES WITH LEADERSHIP STYLES OF EMPLOYEES OF LIC AND CBB VIZ., HIGHER LEVEL EXECUTIVES, MIDDLE LEVEL EXECUTIVES AND LOWER LEVEL EXECUTIVES

Inter-Correlation Between SEOP Variables and Leadership Styles of LIC

Table 9 presents the inter-correlation between socio-economic and organizational position variables and five leadership styles viz., authoritarian, participative, bureaucratic, task-orientation and nurturant for Higher Level Executives of LIC. 'Age' was correlated significantly but negatively with 'nurturant' style ($r = -0.660$, $P<0.05$) indicating that 'nurturant' style decreases with the increase of 'age'.

'Experience' was correlated significantly but negatively with 'bureaucratic' style ($r = -0.787$, $P<0.05$), 'task-orientation' style (r= -0.806, P<0.01), and 'nurturant' style(r= -0.904, P<0.01) indicating that 'bureaucratic', 'task-orientation' and 'nurturant' styles decreases with the higher level of 'experience'.

'Education' was correlated significantly and positively with 'bureaucratic' style (r= -0.767, P<0.05), and 'nurturant' style (r= -0.926, P<0.01) indicating that 'bureaucratic' and 'nurturant' styles increases with the higher level of 'education'.

Table 9
Inter-correlation Between SEOP Variables and Leadership Styles for Higher Level Executives of LIC (N=9)

	Leadership Styles				
SEOP Variables	*Authoritarian*	*Participative*	*Bureaucratic*	*Task orientation*	*Nurturant*
Designation	-0.192	-0.033	0.449	0.134	0.502
Age	-0.080	0.263	-0.590	-0.070	*-0.660
Experience	-0.136	-0.575	*-0.787	**-0.806	**-0.904
Education	-0.405	0.340	*0.767	0.550	**0.926
Economic Status	*0.766	-0.397	0.543	-0.203	0.095

Source: Compiled from field survey

'Economic status' was correlated significantly and positively with 'authoritarian' style (r= 0.766, P<0.0) indicating that authoritarian style increases with the higher level of 'economic status'.

None of the other socio-economic and organizational position variables, however, were found not to be significantly correlated with leadership styles. Hence, the hypothesis, that there is no significant relationship between socio-economic and organizational position variables and leadership styles of employees of LIC is rejected in the case of 'age' vs 'nurturant', 'experience' vs 'bureaucratic', 'experience' vs 'task-orientation', 'experience' vs 'nurturant', 'education' vs 'bureaucratic'and 'education' vs 'nurturant' 'economic status' vs 'authoritarian' and is accepted in all other cases.

INTER CORRELATION BETWEEN SEOP VARIABLES AND LEADERSHIP STYLES OF CBB

Table 10 presents the inter-correlation between socio-economic and organizational position variables and five leadership styles viz., authoritarian, participative, bureaucratic, task-orientation and nurturant for Higher Level Executives of CBB. 'Age' was correlated significantly but negatively with 'authoritarian' style(r= -0.388, P<0.05) and task-orientation style(r= -0.518, P<0.01) indicating that 'authoritarian' and task-orientation style decreases with the increase of 'age'.

'Experience' was correlated significantly but negatively with 'participative' style (r= -0.395, P<0.05) and 'nurturant' style(r= -0.394, P<0.01) indicating that 'participative' and 'nurturant' styles decreases with the higher level of 'experience'.

Table 10
Inter-correlation Between SEOP Variables and Leadership Styles for Higher Level Executives of CBB (N=30)

SEOP Variables	*Leadership Styles*				
	Authoritarian	*Participative*	*Bureaucratic*	*Task orientation*	*Nurturant*
Designation	-0.112	0.217	0.116	0.019	0.160
Age	*-0.388	0.004	0.004	**-0.518	-0.250
Experience	0.051	*-0.395	-0.227	-0.315	*-0.394
Education	**-0.851	0.287	0.164	**-0.570	*-0.457
Economic Status	*-0.448	*0.390	-0.120	0.034	0.119

Source: Compiled from field survey

'Education' was correlated significantly but negatively with 'authoritarian' style (r= -0.851, P<0.01), task-orientation style(r= -0.570, P<0.01) and 'nurturant' style(r= -0.457, P<0.05) indicating that 'authoritarian', task-orientation and 'nurturant' styles decreases with the higher level of 'education'.

'Economic status' was correlated significantly but negatively with 'authoritarian' style (r= -0.448, P<0.05) indicating that authoritarian styles decreases with the higher level of 'economic status'. 'economic status' was also correlated significantly and positively with 'participative' style (r= 0.390, P<0.05) indicating that 'participative' styles increases with the higher level of 'economic status'.

None of the other socio-economic and organizational position variables, however, were found not to be significantly

correlated with leadership styles. Hence, the hypothesis, that there is no significant relationship between socio-economic and organizational position variables and leadership styles of employees of CBB is rejected in the case of 'age' vs 'authoritarian', 'age' vs 'task-orientation', 'experience' vs 'participative', 'experience' vs 'nurturant', 'education' vs 'authoritarian', 'education' vs 'task-orientation' 'education' vs 'nurturant', and 'economic status' vs 'authoritarian' 'economic status' vs 'participative' and is accepted in all other cases.

Comparison of Higher Level Executives of LIC and CBB

In Higher Level Executives of LIC, 'age' was significantly but negatively correlated with 'nurturant' style whereas in Higher Level Executives of CBB, 'age' was significantly but negatively correlated with 'authoritarian' and 'task-orientation' styles. In Higher Level Executives of LIC, 'experience' was significantly but negatively correlated with 'bureaucratic', 'task-orientation' and 'nurturant' style whereas in Higher Level Executives of CBB, 'experience' was significantly but negatively correlated with 'participative' and 'nurturant' styles. In Higher Level Executives of LIC, 'education' was significantly and positively correlated with 'bureaucratic' and 'nurturant' style whereas in Higher Level Executives of CBB, 'education' was significantly but negatively correlated with 'authoritarian', 'task-orientation' and 'nurturant' styles. In Higher Level Executives of LIC, 'economic status' was significantly and positively correlated with 'authoritarian' style whereas in Higher Level Executives of CBB, 'economic status' was significantly but negatively correlated with 'authoritarian' and also 'economic status' was significantly and positively correlated with 'participative' style.

Table 11 presents the inter-correlation between socio-economic and organizational position variables and five leadership styles viz., authoritarian, participative, bureaucratic, task-orientation and nurturant for Middle Level Executives of LIC. 'age' was correlated significantly and positively with 'bureaucratic' style($r = 0.359$, $P<0.05$) indicating that 'bureaucratic' style increases with the higher level of 'age'.

'Education' was correlated significantly and positively with 'nurturant' style(r= 0.284, P<0.05) indicating that 'nurturant' style increases with the higher level of 'education'.

Table 11
Inter-correlation Between SEOP Variables and Leadership Styles for Middle Level Executives of LIC (N=49)

	Leadership Styles				
SEOP Variables	*Authori-tarian*	*Partici-pative*	*Bureau-cratic*	*Task orie-ntation*	*Nurt-urant*
Designation	0.171	0.163	0.105	0.176	0.03
Age	-0.132	0.003	*0.359	0.013	-0.106
Experience	-0.13	-0.181	0.002	0.128	-0.036
Education	0.120	0.067	-0.260	0.084	*0.284
Economic Status	-0.009	0.168	0.262	0.104	-0.133

Source: Compiled from field survey

None of the other socio-economic and organizational position variables, however, were found not to be significantly correlated with leadership styles. Hence, the hypothesis, that there is no significant relationship between socio-economic and organizational position variables and leadership styles of employees of LIC is rejected in the case of 'age' vs 'bureaucratic', and 'education' vs 'nurturant' and is accepted in all other cases.

Table 12
Inter-correlation Between SEOP Variables and Leadership Styles for Middle Level Executives of CBB (N=34)

	Leadership Styles				
SEOP Variables	*Authori-tarian*	*Partici-pative*	*Bureau-cratic*	*Task orie-ntation*	*Nurt-urant*
Designation	-0.142	0.212	-0.308	0.082	-0.032
Age	-0.001	-0.151	-0.152	-0.025	-0.196
Experience	0.017	-0.154	-0.147	-0.051	-0.120
Education	0.193	-0.068	0.128	0.106	0.114
Economic Status	0.081	-0.159	-0.009	0.056	0.018

Source: Compiled from field survey

Table 12 presents the inter-correlation between socio-economic and organizational position variables and five leadership styles viz., authoritarian, participative, bureaucratic, task-orientation and nurturant for Middle Level Executives of CBB.

None of the socio-economic and organizational position variables were found not to be significantly correlated with leadership styles. Hence, the hypothesis, that there is no significant relationship between socio-economic and organizational position variables and leadership styles of employees of CBB is accepted.

Comparison of Middle Level Executives of LIC and CBB

In Middle Level Executives of LIC and CBB, 'age' was significantly and positively correlated with 'bureaucratic' style whereas in Middle Level Executives of CBB, 'age' does not correlate significantly with any leadership style. In Middle Level Executives of LIC and CBB, 'education' was significantly and positively correlated with 'nurturant' style whereas in Middle Level Executives of CBB, 'education' does not correlate significantly with any leadership style.

Table 13
Inter-correlation Between SEOP Variables and Leadership Styles for Lower Level Executives of LIC (N=40)

	Leadership Styles				
SEOP Variables	*Authoritarian*	*Participative*	*Bureaucratic*	*Task orientation*	*Nurturant*
Designation	0.223	-0.026	0.031	-0.090	-0.099
Age	-0.033	-0.066	-0.281	-0.293	-0.241
Experience	-0.122	-0.157	-0.285	**-0.580	-0.680
Education	-0.230	*0.327	*-0.387	-0.095	-0.073
Economic Status	0.250	-0.107	-0.180	*-0.319	*-0.339

Source: Compiled from field survey

Table 13 presents the inter-correlation between socio-economic and organizational position variables and five leadership styles viz., authoritarian, participative, bureaucratic, task-orientation and nurturant for Lower Level Executives of LIC. 'experience' was correlated significantly but negatively with 'task-orientation' style (r= -0.580, P<0.01), indicating that 'task-orientation' style decreases with the higher level of 'experience'.

'Education' was correlated significantly and positively with 'participative' style (r= 0.327, P<0.05), indicating that participative style increases with the higher level of 'education'. 'education' was correlated significantly but negatively with 'bureaucratic' style (r= -0.387, P<0.05), indicating that 'bureaucratic' style decreases with the higher level of 'education'.

'Economic status' was correlated significantly but negatively with 'task-orientation' style (r= -0.319, P<0.05) and 'nurturant' style (r= -0.339, P<0.05) indicating that 'task-orientation' and 'nurturant' styles decreases with the higher level of 'economic status'.

None of the other socio-economic and organizational position variables, however, were found not to be significantly correlated with leadership styles. Hence, the hypothesis, that there is no significant relationship between socio-economic and organizational position variables and leadership styles of employees of LIC is rejected in the case of 'experience' vs 'task-orientation', 'education' vs 'participative', 'education' vs 'bureaucratic' 'economic status' vs 'task-orientation' 'economic status' vs 'nurturant' and is accepted in all other cases.

Table 14
Inter-correlation Between SEOP Variables and Leadership Styles for Lower Level Executives of CBB (N=107)

	Leadership Styles				
SEOP Variables	*Authori-tarian*	*Partici-pative*	*Bureau-cratic*	*Task orie-ntation*	*Nurt-urant*
Designation	0.113	-0.055	0.006	-0.172	0.058
Age	-0.101	-0.144	-0.058	0.083	0.119
Experience	0.058	-0.138	0.024	0.026	0.155
Education	-0.159	-0.153	-0.161	-0.063	-0.112
Economic Status	0.113	*-0.233	-0.126	0.078	0.078

Source: Compiled from field survey

Table 14 presents the inter-correlation between socio-economic and organizational position variables and five leadership styles viz., authoritarian, participative, bureaucratic, task-orientation and nurturant for Lower Level Executives of CBB.

'Economic status' was correlated significantly but negatively with 'participative' style (r= -0.233, P<0.05) indicating that participative style decreases with the higher level of 'economic status'.

None of the socio-economic and organizational position variables were found not to be significantly correlated with leadership styles. Hence, the hypothesis, that there is no significant relationship between socio-economic and organizational position variables and leadership styles of employees of CBB is rejected in the case of 'economic status' vs 'participative' and is accepted in all other cases.

Comparison of Lower Level Executives of LIC and CBB

In Lower Level Executives of LIC, 'experience' was significantly but negatively correlated with 'task-orientation' style whereas in Lower Level Executives of CBB, 'experience' does not correlate significantly with any leadership style. In Lower Level Executives of LIC, 'education' was significantly and positively correlated with 'participative' style and also 'education' was significantly but negatively correlated with 'bureaucratic' style whereas in Lower Level Executives of CBB, 'experience' does not correlate significantly with any leadership style. In Lower Level Executives of LIC, 'economic status' was significantly but negatively correlated with 'task-orientation' and 'nurturant' style whereas in Lower Level Executives of CBB, 'economic status' was significantly but negatively correlated with 'participative' style.

INTER-CORRELATION OF LEADERSHIP STYLES OF EMPLOYEES OF LIC AND CBB VIZ., HIGHER LEVEL EXECUTIVES, MIDDLE LEVEL EXECUTIVES AND LOWER LEVEL EXECUTIVES

Inter-Correlation of Leadership Styles of LIC

Table 15 presents the inter-correlations among leadership styles of Higher Level Executives of LIC. The 'participative' style was correlated significantly and positively with 'task-orientation' style(r=0.928, P<0.01) indicating that 'task-orientation' style increases with the greater role of 'participative' style

The 'bureaucratic' style was significantly and positively correlated with 'nurturant' style(r=0.712, P<0.05) indicating that 'nurturant' style increases with the higher role of 'bureaucratic' style.

Table 15
Inter-correlation of Leadership Styles for Higher Level Executives of LIC (N=9)

Leadership Styles	*Authoritarian*	*Participative*	*Bureaucratic*	*Task orientation*	*Nurturant*
Authoritarian		-0.339	0.013	-0.208	-0.238
Participative			0.330	**0.928	0.547
Bureaucratic				0.464	*0.712
Task-orientation					*0.783
Nurturant					

Source: Compiled from field survey

The 'task-orientation' style was significantly and positively correlated with 'nurturant' style(r=0.783, P<0.05) indicating that 'nurturant' style increases with the higher role of 'task-orientation' style. Hence, the hypothesis, that there is no significant relationship among leadership styles of employees of LIC is rejected in the case of 'participative' vs 'task-orientation', 'bureaucratic' vs 'nurturant' and 'task-orientation' vs 'nurturant' styles and is accepted in all other cases.

Intercorrelation of Leadership Styles of CBB

Table 16 presents the inter-correlations among leadership styles of Higher Level Executives of CBB. The 'authoritarian' style was correlated significantly but negatively with 'participative' style(r= -0.429, P<0.05) indicating that 'participative' style decreases with the higher role of 'authoritarian' style. The 'authoritarian' style was also correlated significantly and positively with 'task-orientation' style(r= 0.420, P<0.05) and 'nurturant' style(r= 0.384, P<0.05) indicating that 'task-orientation' and 'nurturant' styles increases with the greater role of 'authoritarian' style.

The 'participative' style was correlated significantly and positively with 'task-orientation' style(r=0.415, P<0.05) and with 'nurturant' style (r=0.582, P<0.01) indicating that 'task-orientation' and 'nurturant' styles increases with the greater adoption of 'participative' style.

Table 16
Inter-correlation of Leadership Styles for Higher Level Executives of CBB (N=30)

Leadership Styles	*Authoritarian*	*Participative*	*Bureaucratic*	*Task orientation*	*Nurturant*
Authoritarian		*-0.429	-0.036	*0.420	*0.384
Participative			0.183	*0.415	**0.582
Bureaucratic				**0.465	0.112
Task-orientation					**0.730
Nurturant					

Source: Compiled from field survey

The 'bureaucratic' style was correlated significantly and positively with 'task-orientation' style(r=0.465, P<0.01) indicating that 'task-orientation' style increases with the greater role of 'bureaucratic' style.

The 'task-orientation' style was correlated significantly and positively with 'nurturant' style(r=0.730, P<0.01) indicating that 'nurturant' style increases with the greater role of 'task-orientation' style. Hence, the hypothesis, that there is no significant relationship among leadership styles of employees of CBB is rejected in the case of 'authoritarian' vs 'participative', 'authoritarian' vs 'task-orientation', 'authoritarian' vs 'nurturant', 'participative' vs 'task-orientation', 'participative' vs 'nurturant', 'bureaucratic' vs 'task orientation', and 'task-orientation' vs 'nurturant' and is accepted in all other cases.

Comparison of Higher Level Executives of LIC and CBB

In Higher Level Executives of LIC, 'authoritarian' style does not correlate significantly with other leadership styles whereas in Higher Level Executives of CBB, 'authoritarian' style was significantly but negatively correlated with 'participative' style and also 'authoritarian' style was significantly and positively correlated with task orientation and 'nurturant' styles. In Higher Level Executives of LIC, 'participative' style was significantly and positively correlated with 'task-orientation' style whereas in Higher Level Executives of CBB, 'participative' style was significantly and positively correlated with 'task-orientation' and 'nurturant' styles. In Higher Level Executives of LIC, 'bureaucratic' style was significantly and positively correlated with 'nurturant' style whereas in Higher Level Executives of CBB, 'bureaucratic' style was significantly and positively correlated with 'task-orientation' styles. In Higher Level Executives of LIC and CBB, 'task-orientation' style was significantly and positively correlated with 'nurturant' style.

Table 17
Inter-correlation of Leadership Styles for Middle Level Executives of LIC (N=49)

Leadership Styles	*Authoritarian*	*Participative*	*Bureaucratic*	*Task orientation*	*Nurturant*
Authoritarian		0.006	*0.310	0.123	*-0.361
Participative			0.254	0.207	*0.357
Bureaucratic				**0.455	0.143
Task-orientation					**0.466
Nurturant					

Source: Compiled from field survey

Table 17 presents the inter-correlations among leadership styles for Middle Level Executives of LIC. The 'authoritarian' style was correlated significantly and positively with 'bureaucratic' style($r=0.310$, $P<0.05$) indicating that 'bureaucratic' style increases with the higher role of 'authoritarian' style. 'authoritarian' style was also correlated significantly but negatively with 'nurturant' style($r= -0.361$, $P<0.05$) indicating that 'bureaucratic' style decreases with the increase of 'authoritarian' style.

The 'participative' style was correlated significantly and positively with 'nurturant' style($r=0.357$, $P<0.05$) indicating that 'nurturant' style increases with the greater role of 'participative' style.

The 'bureaucratic' style was significantly and positively correlated with 'task-orientation' style(r=0.455, P<0.01) indicating that 'task-orientation' style increases with the increase of 'bureaucratic' style.

The 'task-orientation' style was significantly and positively correlated with 'nurturant' style(r=0.466, P<0.01) indicating that 'nurturant' style increases with the higher role of 'task-orientation' style. Hence, the hypothesis, that there is no significant relationship among leadership styles of employees of LIC is rejected in the case of 'authoritarian' vs 'bureaucratic', 'authoritarian' vs 'nurturant', 'participative' vs 'nurturant', 'bureaucratic' vs 'task-orientation' and 'task-orientation' vs 'nurturant' styles and is accepted in all other cases.

Table 18
Inter-correlation of Leadership Styles for Middle Level Executives of CBB (N=34)

Leadership Styles	*Authoritarian*	*Participative*	*Bureaucratic*	*Task orientation*	*Nurturant*
Authoritarian		-0.076	**0.736	0.260	**0.494
Participative			0.267	**0.566	*0.406
Bureaucratic				**0.501	**0.674
Task-orientation					**0.747
Nurturant					

Source: Compiled from field survey

Table 18 presents the inter-correlations among leadership styles of Middle Level Executives of CBB. The 'authoritarian' style was correlated significantly and positively with 'bureaucratic' style(r= 0.736, P<0.01) and 'nurturant' style (r= 0.494, P<0.01) indicating that 'bureaucratic' and 'nurturant' styles increases with the greater role of 'authoritarian' style.

The 'participative' style was correlated significantly and positively with 'task-orientation' style(r=0.566, P<0.01) and with 'nurturant' style(r=0.406, P<0.05) indicating that 'task-orientation' and 'nurturant' styles increases with the higher role of 'participative' style.

The 'bureaucratic' style was correlated significantly and positively with 'task-orientation' style(r=0.501, P<0.01) and with 'nurturant' style(r=0.674, P<0.01) indicating that 'task-orientation' and 'nurturant' styles increases with the higher role of 'bureaucratic' style.

The 'task-orientation' style was correlated significantly and positively with 'nurturant' style(r=0.747, P<0.01) indicating that 'nurturant' style increases with the increase of 'task-orientation' style. Hence, the hypothesis, that there is no significant relationship among leadership styles of employees of CBB is rejected in the case of 'authoritarian' vs 'bureaucratic', 'authoritarian' vs 'nurturant', 'participative' vs 'task-orientation', 'participative' vs 'nurturant', 'bureaucratic' vs 'task-orientation', 'bureaucratic' vs 'nurturant', and 'task-orientation' vs 'nurturant' and is accepted in all other cases.

Comparison of Middle Level Executives of LIC and CBB

In Middle Level Executives of LIC, 'authoritarian' style was significantly and positively correlated with 'bureaucratic' style and also 'authoritarian' style was significantly but negatively correlated with 'nurturant' style whereas in Middle Level Executives of CBB, 'authoritarian' style was significantly and positively correlated with 'bureaucratic' and 'nurturant' style. In Middle Level Executives of LIC and CBB, 'participative' style was significantly and positively correlated with 'task orientation' style. In Middle Level Executives of LIC, 'participative' style does not correlate significantly with 'bureaucratic' and 'task orientation' styles whereas in Middle Level Executives of CBB, 'participative' style was significantly and positively correlated with 'task-orientation' and 'nurturant' styles. In Middle Level Executives of LIC, 'bureaucratic' style was significantly and positively correlated with 'task-orientation' style whereas in Middle Level Executives of CBB, 'bureaucratic' style was significantly and positively correlated with 'task-orientation' and 'nurturant' styles. In Middle Level Executives of LIC and CBB, 'task-orientation' style was significantly and positively correlated with 'nurturant' style.

Table 19
Inter-correlation of Leadership Styles for Lower Level Executives of LIC (N=40)

Leadership Styles	*Authori-tarian*	*Partici-pative*	*Bureau-cratic*	*Task orie-ntation*	*Nurt-urant*
Authoritarian		0.181	**0.729	**0.498	**0.439
Participative			0.140	**0.492	*0.368
Bureaucratic				**0.587	**0.490
Task-orientation					**0.831
Nurturant					

Source: Compiled from field survey.

Table 19 presents the inter-correlations among leadership styles of Lower Level Executives of LIC. The 'authoritarian' style was correlated significantly and positively with 'bureaucratic' style(r= 0.729, P<0.01) 'task-orientation' style(r= 0.498, P<0.01) and 'nurturant' style (r=0.439, P<0.05) indicating that 'bureaucratic', 'task-orientation' and 'nurturant' styles increases with the higher role of 'authoritarian' style.

The 'participative' style was correlated significantly and positively with 'task-orientation' style(r=0.492, P<0.01) and with 'nurturant' style(r=0.368, P<0.05) indicating that 'task-orientation' and 'nurturant' styles increases with the higher level of 'participative' style.

The 'bureaucratic' style was correlated significantly and positively with 'task-orientation' style(r=0.587, P<0.01) and with 'nurturant' style(r=0.490, P<0.05) indicating that 'task-orientation' and 'nurturant' styles increases with the increase of 'bureaucratic' style.

The 'task-orientation' style was correlated significantly and positively with 'nurturant' style(r=0.831, P<0.01) indicating that 'nurturant' style increases with the increase of 'task-orientation' style. Hence, the hypothesis, that there is no significant relationship among leadership styles of employees of LIC is rejected in the case of 'authoritarian' vs 'bureaucratic', 'authoritarian' vs 'task-orientation', 'authoritarian' vs 'nurturant', 'participative' vs 'task-orientation', 'participative' vs 'nurturant', 'bureaucratic' vs 'task-orientation', 'bureaucratic' vs 'nurturant', and 'task-orientation' vs 'nurturant' and is accepted in all other cases.

Table 20
Inter-correlation of Leadership Styles for Lower Level Executives of CBB (N=107)

Leadership Styles	*Authori-tarian*	*Partici-pative*	*Bureau-cratic*	*Task orie-ntation*	*Nurt-urant*
Authoritarian		0.060	*0.193	-0.106	0.081
Participative			**0.276	*0.239	*0.237
Bureaucratic				**0.283	-0.018
Task-orientation					**0.311
Nurturant					

Source: Compiled from field survey

Table 20 presents the inter-correlations among leadership styles of lower level executives of CBB. The 'authoritarian' style was correlated significantly and positively with 'bureaucratic' style(r= 0.193, P<0.05) indicating that 'bureaucratic' style increases with the increase of 'authoritarian' style.

The 'participative' style was correlated significantly and positively with 'bureaucratic' style(r=0.276, P<0.01) 'task-orientation' style(r=0.239, P<0.05) and with 'nurturant' style(r=0.237, P<0.05) indicating that 'bureaucratic', 'task-orientation' and 'nurturant' styles increases with the higher level of 'participative' style.

The 'bureaucratic' style was correlated significantly and positively with 'task-orientation' style(r=0.283, P<0.01) indicating that 'task-orientation' style increases with the increase of 'bureaucratic' style.

The 'task-orientation' style was correlated significantly and positively with 'nurturant' style(r=0.311, P<0.01) indicating that 'nurturant' style increases with the increase of 'task-orientation' style. Hence, the hypothesis, that there is no significant relationship among leadership styles of employees of CBB is rejected in the case of 'authoritarian' vs 'bureaucratic 'participative' vs 'bureaucratic' 'participative' vs 'task-orientation', 'participative' vs 'nurturant', 'bureaucratic' vs 'task-orientation', and 'task-orientation' vs 'nurturant' and is accepted in all other cases.

Comparison of Lower Level Executives of LIC and CBB

In Lower Level Executives of LIC, 'authoritarian' style was significantly and positively correlated with 'bureaucratic', 'task-orientation' and 'nurturant' styles whereas in Junior Level Executives of CBB, 'authoritarian' style was significantly and positively correlated with 'bureaucratic' styles. In Lower Level Executives of LIC, 'participative' style was significantly and positively correlated with 'task-orientation' and 'nurturant' styles whereas in Junior Level Executives of CBB, 'participative' style was significantly and positively correlated with 'bureaucratic', 'task-orientation' and 'nurturant' styles. In Lower Level Executives of LIC, 'bureaucratic' style was significantly and positively correlated with 'task-orientation' and 'nurturant' styles whereas in Junior Level Executives of CBB, 'bureaucratic' style was significantly and positively correlated with 'task-orientation' style. In Junior Level Executives of LIC and CBB, 'task-orientation' style was significantly and positively correlated with 'nurturant' style.

5

SUBORDINATES PERCEPTION OF LEADERSHIP IN INSURANCE AND BANKING SECTOR

INTRODUCTION

The organizational effectiveness and leadership effectiveness are well-knit to each other. In other words the performance of the people is based on their perceptions about themselves, their superiors and subordinates. These perceptions decide the quality of interpersonal relations among the managers in their leadership role while dealing with their subordinates. Similarly the subordinates accept their leaders basing on the styles they adopt.

This chapter presents the leadership styles perceived by subordinates viz., Middle Level Executives, Lower Level Executives and Clerks of LIC and CBB.

The correlations of socio-economic and organizational position variables with leadership styles were computed. Following this, correlations were computed among five leadership styles viz., authoritarian, participative, bureaucratic, task-orientation and nurturant.

In this chapter the presentation and discussion of the data pertain to the following:

I. Relationship of SEOP variables with leadership styles for employees of LIC and CBB viz., Middle Level Executives, Lower Level Executives and Clerks.

II. Inter-correlation of leadership styles for employees of LIC and CBB viz., Middle Level Executives, Lower Level Executives and Clerks.

INTER-CORRELATION BETWEEN SEOP VARIABLES AND LEADERSHIP STYLES

Table 1 presents the inter-correlation between socio-economic and organizational position variables and five leadership styles of Middle Level Executives of LIC. 'experience' was significantly and positively correlated with 'participative' style (r= 0.439, p<0.01), 'bureaucratic' style (r= -0.286, p<0.05) and 'nurturant' style (r= 0.507, p<0.05), indicating that 'participative', 'bureaucratic' and 'nurturant' styles increases with the higher level of 'experience'.

Table 1
Inter-correlation Between SEOP Variables and Leadership Styles of Middle Level Executives of LIC (N=49)

	Leadership Styles				
SEOP Variables	*Authori-tarian*	*Partici-pative*	*Bureau-cratic*	*Task orie-ntation*	*Nurt-urant*
Designation	0.223	-0.009	0.149	0.203	0.049
Age	0.152	0.021	-0.154	0.065	0.153
Experience	-0.013	**0.439	*0.286	0.244	**0.507
Education	-0.247	-0.070	0.042	-0.072	-0.153
Economic Status	0.128	*0.334	0.275	-0.027	-0.086

Source: Compiled from field survey

'Economic status' was significantly and positively correlated with 'participative' style (r= 0.334, p<0.05), indicating that 'participative' style increases with the higher level of 'economic status'.

None of the other socio-economic and organizational position variables, however, were found not to be significantly correlated with leadership styles. Hence, the hypothesis, that there is no significant relationship between socio-economic and organisational position variables and leadership styles of employees of LIC is rejected in the case of 'experience' vs 'participative' style, 'experience' vs 'bureaucratic' style, 'experience' vs 'nurturant' style, 'economic status' vs 'participative' and is accepted in all other cases.

Table 2 presents the inter-correlation between socio-economic and organizational position variables and five leadership styles viz., authoritarian, participative, bureaucratic, task-orientation and nurturant for Middle Level Executives of CBB. 'experience' was correlated significantly and positively with 'participative' style (r= 0.358, P<0.05) indicating that 'participative' style increases with the higher level of 'experience'.

Table 2
Inter-correlation Between SEOP Variables and Leadership Styles of Middle Level Executives of CBB (N=34)

SEOP Variables	*Leadership Styles*				
	Authoritarian	*Participative*	*Bureaucratic*	*Task orientation*	*Nurturant*
Designation	-0.022	0.156	0.170	-0.072	0.218
Age	-0.244	0.331	0.229	0.157	0.199
Experience	-0.155	*0.358	0.261	0.225	0.250
Education	-0.041	-0.033	-0.067	0.189	0.091
Economic Status	0.012	0.068	0.039	0.127	0.112

Source: Compiled from field survey

None of the other socio-economic and organizational position variables, however, were found not to be significantly correlated with leadership styles. Hence, the hypothesis, that there is no significant relationship between socio-economic and organizational position variables and leadership styles of employees of CBB is rejected in the case of 'experience' vs 'participative', and is accepted in all other cases.

Comparison of Middle Level Executives of LIC and CBB

In Middle Level Executives of LIC, 'experience' was significantly and positively correlated with 'participative', 'bureaucratic' and 'nurturant' styles whereas in Middle Level Executives of CBB, 'experience' was significantly and positively correlated with 'participative' style. In Middle Level Executives of LIC, 'economic status' was significantly and positively correlated with 'participative' style whereas in Middle Level Executives of CBB, 'economic status' does not correlate significantly with any leadership style.

Table 3
Inter-correlation Between SEOP Variables and Leadership Styles of Lower Level Executives of LIC (N=40)

	Leadership Styles				
SEOP Variables	*Authori-tarian*	*Partici-pative*	*Bureau-cratic*	*Task orie-ntation*	*Nurt-urant*
Designation	*0.365	-0.057	-0.083	-0.142	0.068
Age	-0.050	*-0.410	-0.126	*-0.411	*-0.345
Experience	0.147	**-0.438	**-0.597	-0.298	-0.179
Education	0.194	0.165	*0.343	0.143	0.204
Economic Status	-0.225	-0.225	0.048	-0.258	-0.215

Source: Compiled from field survey

Table 3 presents the inter-correlation between socio-economic and organizational position variables and five leadership styles of Lower Level Executives of LIC. The correlation between 'designation' and 'authoritarian' style of leadership was found to be significantly positive($r= 0.365$, $P<0.05$) indicating that the 'authoritarian' style increases with the higher level of 'designation'.

'Age' was significantly but negatively correlated with 'participative' style ($r= -0.410$, $p<0.05$) 'task-orientation' style ($r= -0.411$, $p<0.05$) and 'nurturant' style ($r= -0.345$, $p<0.05$)indicating that 'participative', 'task-orientation' and 'nurturant' styles decreases with the higher level of 'age'.

'Experience' was significantly but negatively correlated with 'participative' style ($r= -0.438$, $p<0.01$) and 'bureaucratic' style ($r= -0.597$, $p<0.01$) indicating that 'participative' and 'bureaucratic' styles decreases with the increase of 'experience'.

The correlation between 'education' and 'bureaucratic' style of leadership was found to be significantly positive($r= 0.343$, $P<0.05$) indicating that the 'bureaucratic' style increases with the higher level of 'education'.

None of the other socio-economic and organisational position variables, however, were found not to be significantly correlated with leadership styles. Hence, the hypothesis, that there is no significant relationship between socio-economic and organisational position variables and leadership styles of employees of LIC is rejected in the case of 'designation' vs 'authoritarian', 'age' vs 'participative', 'age' vs 'task-orientation', 'age' vs 'nurturant', 'experience' vs 'participative', 'experience' vs 'bureaucratic' style, and 'education' vs 'bureaucratic' style and is accepted in all other cases.

Table 4
Inter-correlation Between SEOP Variables and Leadership Styles of Lower Level Executives of CBB (N=107)

	Leadership Styles				
SEOP Variables	*Authori-tarian*	*Partici-pative*	*Bureau-cratic*	*Task orie-ntation*	*Nurt-urant*
Designation	0.092	0.118	0.075	0.046	0.005
Age	-0.067	0.071	0.134	-0.061	-0.010
Experience	0.052	0.080	0.180	-0.047	-0.010
Education	-0.053	-0.043	*-0.201	*0.241	-0.114
Economic Status	0.026	**0.297	-0.043	0.041	0.102

Source: Compiled from field survey

Table 4 presents the inter-correlation between socio-economic and organizational position variables and five leadership styles viz., authoritarian, participative, bureaucratic, task-orientation and nurturant for Higher Level Executives of CBB. 'education' was correlated significantly but negatively with 'bureaucratic' style (r= -0.201, P<0.05) indicating that 'bureaucratic' style decreases with the increase of 'education'. 'education' was also correlated significantly and positively with 'task-orientation' style (r= 0.241, P<0.05) indicating that 'task-orientation' style increases with the increase of 'education'.

'Economic status' was correlated significantly and positively with 'participative' style (r= 0.297, P<0.01) indicating that participative style increases with the increase of 'economic status'.

None of the other socio-economic and organizational position variables, however, were found not to be significantly

correlated with leadership styles. Hence, the hypothesis, that there is no significant relationship between socio-economic and organizational position variables and leadership styles of employees of CBB is rejected in the case of 'education' vs 'bureaucratic', 'education' vs 'task-orientation', 'economic status' vs 'participative' and is accepted in all other cases.

Comparison of Lower Level Executives of LIC and CBB

In Lower Level Executives of LIC, 'designation' was significantly and positively correlated with 'authoritarian' style whereas in Lower Level Executives of CBB, 'designation' does not correlate significantly with any leadership style. In Lower Level Executives of LIC, 'age' was significantly but negatively correlated with 'participative', 'task-orientation' and 'nurturant' styles whereas in Lower Level Executives of CBB, 'age' does not correlate significantly with any leadership style. In Lower Level Executives of LIC, 'experience' was significantly but negatively correlated with 'participative' and 'bureaucratic' styles whereas in Lower Level Executives of CBB, 'experience' does not correlate significantly with any leadership style. In Lower Level Executives of LIC, 'education' was significantly and positively correlated with 'bureaucratic' style whereas in Lower Level Executives of CBB, 'education' was significantly but negatively correlated with 'bureaucratic' style and also 'education' was significantly and positively correlated with 'task-orientation' style. In Lower Level Executives of LIC, 'economic status' does not correlate significantly with any leadership style whereas in Lower Level Executives of CBB, 'economic status' was significantly and positively correlated with 'participative' style.

Table 5 presents the inter-correlation between socio-economic and organizational position variables and five leadership styles of LIC. The correlation between 'designation' and 'authoritarian' style of leadership was found to be significantly negative($r= -0.147$, $P<0.05$) indicating that the 'authoritarian' style decreases with the higher level of 'designation'.

Table 5
Inter-correlation Between SEOP Variables and Leadership Styles of Clerks of LIC (N=202)

SEOP Variables	*Leadership Styles*				
	Authori-tarian	*Partici-pative*	*Bureau-cratic*	*Task orie-ntation*	*Nurt-urant*
Designation	*-0.147	0.026	-0.075	0.016	0.013
Age	0.096	0.054	-0.028	-0.018	0.054
Experience	0.057	-0.025	**-0.204	-0.026	-0.016
Education	0.017	0.039	-0.040	-0.027	0.117
Economic Status	0.107	0.119	0.011	0.127	0.118

Source: Compiled from field survey

'Experience' was significantly but negatively correlated with 'bureaucratic' style (r= -0.204, p<0.05) indicating that 'bureaucratic' style decreases with the increase of 'experience'.

None of the other socio-economic and organisational position variables, however, were found not to be significantly correlated with leadership styles. Hence, the hypothesis, that there is no significant relationship between socio-economic and organisational position variables and leadership styles of employees of LIC is rejected in the case of 'designation' vs 'authoritarian', and 'experience' vs 'bureaucratic' style, and is accepted in all other cases.

Table 6
Inter-correlation Between SEOP Variables and Leadership Styles of Clerks of CBB (N=329)

SEOP Variables	*Leadership Styles*				
	Authori-tarian	*Partici-pative*	*Bureau-cratic*	*Task orie-ntation*	*Nurt-urant*
Designation	0.038	0.085	0.074	-0.030	0.012
Age	-0.030	-0.056	0.809	**0.249	-0.101
Experience	0.066	-0.026	-0.107	**0.240	-0.034
Education	*-0.128	*-0.136	-0.085	-0.094	*-0.152
Economic Status	0.049	0.041	0.001	0.048	0.027

Source: Compiled from field survey

Table 6 presents the inter-correlation between socio-economic and organizational position variables and five leadership styles viz., authoritarian, participative, bureaucratic, task-orientation and nurturant for Clerks of CBB. 'age' was correlated significantly and positively with 'task-orientation' style(r= 0.249, P<0.01) indicating that 'task-orientation' style increases with the increase of 'age'.

'Experience' was correlated significantly and positively with 'task-orientation' style (r= 0.240, P<0.01) indicating that 'task-orientation' style increases with the higher level of 'experience'.

'Education' was correlated significantly but negatively with 'authoritarian' style (r= -0.128, P<0.05) 'participative' style (r= -0.136, P<0.05) and 'nurturant' style(r= -0.152, P<0.05) indicating that 'authoritarian', participative and 'nurturant' styles decreases with the increase of 'education'.

None of the other socio-economic and organizational position variables, however, were found not to be significantly correlated with leadership styles. Hence, the hypothesis, that there is no significant relationship between socio-economic and organizational position variables and leadership styles of employees of CBB is rejected in the case of 'age' vs 'task-orientation', 'experience' vs 'task-orientation', 'education' vs 'authoritarian' 'education' vs 'participative' and 'education' vs 'nurturant', and is accepted in all other cases.

Comparison of Clerks of LIC and CBB

In Clerks of LIC, 'designation' was significantly but negatively correlated with 'authoritarian' style whereas in Clerks of CBB, 'designation' does not correlate significantly with any leadership style. In Clerks of LIC, 'age' does not correlate significantly with any leadership style whereas in Clerks of CBB, 'age' was significantly and positively correlated with 'task-orientation' style. In Clerks of LIC, 'experience' was significantly but negatively correlated with 'bureaucratic' style. whereas in Clerks of CBB, 'experience' was significantly and positively correlated with 'task-orientation' style. In Clerks of LIC, 'education' does not correlate significantly with any leadership style whereas in Clerks of CBB, 'education' was significantly but negatively correlated with 'authoritarian', 'participative' and 'nurturant' styles.

INTER-CORRELATION OF LEADERSHIP STYLES FOR EMPLOYEES OF LIC AND CBB VIZ., MIDDLE LEVEL EXECUTIVES, LOWER LEVEL EXECUTIVES AND CLERKS

Table 7 presents the inter-correlations among leadership styles of Middle Level Executives of LIC. The 'authoritarian' style was correlated significantly but negatively with 'participative' style (r= -0.387, P<0.01) indicating that 'participative' style decreases with the increase of 'authoritarian' style.

Table 7
Inter-correlation of Leadership Styles for Middle Level Executives of LIC (N=49)

Leadership Styles	*Authoritarian*	*Participative*	*Bureaucratic*	*Task orientation*	*Nurturant*
Authoritarian		**-0.387	0.209	0.085	-0.128
Participative			**0.458	**0.448	**0.681
Bureaucratic				**0.541	**0.646
Task-orientation					**0.861
Nurturant					

Source: Compiled from field survey

The 'participative' style was correlated significantly and positively with 'bureaucratic' style(r=0.458, P<0.01), 'task-orientation' style(r=0.448, P<0.01) and with 'nurturant' style(r=0.681, P<0.01) indicating that 'bureaucratic', 'task-orientation' and 'nurturant' styles increases with the higher level of 'participative' style.

The 'bureaucratic' style was correlated significantly and positively with 'task-orientation' style(r=0.541, P<0.01) and with 'nurturant' style(r=0.646, P<0.01) indicating that 'task-orientation' and 'nurturant' styles increases with the increase of 'bureaucratic' style.

The 'task-orientation' style was correlated significantly and positively with 'nurturant' style(r=0.861, P<0.01) indicating that 'nurturant' styles increases with the increase of 'task-orientation' style. Hence, the hypothesis, that there is no significant relationship among leadership styles of employees of LIC is rejected in the case of 'authoritarian' vs 'participative', 'participative vs 'bureaucratic', 'participative' vs 'task-orientation', 'participative' vs 'nurturant', 'bureaucratic' vs 'task-orientation', 'bureaucratic' vs 'nurturant', and 'task-orientation' vs 'nurturant' and is accepted in all other cases.

Table 8
Inter-correlation of Leadership Styles for Middle Level Executives of CBB (N=34)

Leadership Styles	*Authori-tarian*	*Partici-pative*	*Bureau-cratic*	*Task orie-ntation*	*Nurt-urant*
Authoritarian		0.037	0.065	*-0.366	-0.273
Participative			**0.863	**0.499	**0.812
Bureaucratic				**0.567	**0.780
Task-orientation					**0.683
Nurturant					

Source: Compiled from field survey

Table 8 presents the inter-correlations among leadership styles of Middle Level Executives of CBB. The 'authoritarian' style was correlated significantly but negatively with 'task-orientation' style(r= -0.366, P<0.05) indicating that 'task-orientation' style decreases with the increase of 'authoritarian' style.

The 'participative' style was correlated significantly and positively with 'bureaucratic' style(r=0.863, P<0.01) 'task-orientation' style(r=0.499, P<0.01) and with 'nurturant' style(r=0.812, P<0.01) indicating that 'bureaucratic', 'task-orientation' and 'nurturant' styles increases with the increase of 'participative' style.

The 'bureaucratic' style was correlated significantly and positively with 'task-orientation' style(r=0.567, P<0.01) and with 'nurturant' style(r=0.780, P<0.01) indicating that 'task-orientation' and 'nurturant' styles increases with the increase of 'bureaucratic' style.

The 'task-orientation' style was correlated significantly and positively with 'nurturant' style(r=0.683, P<0.01) indicating that 'nurturant' style increases with the increase of 'task-orientation' style. Hence, the hypothesis, that there is no significant relationship among leadership styles of employees of CBB is rejected in the case of 'authoritarian' vs 'task-orientation', 'participative' vs 'bureaucratic', 'participative' vs 'task-orientation', 'participative' vs 'nurturant', 'bureaucratic' vs 'task-orientation', 'bureaucratic' vs 'nurturant' and 'task-orientation' vs 'nurturant' and is accepted in all other cases.

Comparison of Middle Level Executives of LIC and CBB

In Middle Level Executives of LIC, 'authoritarian' style was significantly but negatively correlated with 'participative' style whereas in Middle Level Executives of CBB, 'authoritarian' style was significantly but negatively correlated with 'task-orientation' style. In Middle Level Executives of LIC and CBB, 'participative' style was significantly and positively correlated with 'bureaucratic', 'task-orientation' and 'nurturant' style. In Middle Level Executives of LIC and CBB, 'bureaucratic' style was significantly and positively correlated with 'task-orientation' and 'nurturant' style. In Middle Level Executives of LIC and CBB, 'task-orientation' style was significantly and positively correlated with 'nurturant' style.

Table 9
Inter-correlation of Leadership Styles for Lower Level Executives of LIC (N=40)

Leadership Styles	*Authoritarian*	*Participative*	*Bureaucratic*	*Task orientation*	*Nurturant*
Authoritarian		0.283	-0.174	*0.324	**0.598
Participative			0.031	**0.887	**0.629
Bureaucratic				-0.131	-0.151
Task-orientation					**0.662
Nurturant					

Source: Compiled from field survey

Table 9 presents the inter-correlations among leadership styles of Lower Level Executives of LIC. The authoritarian' style was correlated significantly and positively with 'task-orientation' style(r=0.324, P<0.05) and with 'nurturant' style(r=0.598, P<0.01) indicating that 'task-orientation' and 'nurturant' styles increases with the higher level of 'authoritarian' style.

The 'participative' style was correlated significantly and positively with 'task-orientation' style(r=0.887, P<0.01) and with 'nurturant' style(r=0.629, P<0.01) indicating that 'task-orientation' and 'nurturant' styles increases with the increase of 'participative' style.

The 'task-orientation' style was correlated significantly and positively with 'nurturant' style(r=0.662, P<0.01) indicating that 'nurturant' styles increases with the increase of 'task-orientation' style. Hence, the hypothesis, that there is no significant relationship among leadership styles of employees of LIC is rejected in the case of 'authoritarian' vs 'task-orientation', 'authoritarian' vs 'nurturant', 'participative' vs 'task-orientation', 'participative' vs 'nurturant', and 'task-orientation' vs 'nurturant' and is accepted in all other cases.

Table 10
Inter-correlation of Leadership Styles for Lower Level Executives of CBB (N=107)

Leadership Styles	*Authoritarian*	*Participative*	*Bureaucratic*	*Task orientation*	*Nurturant*
Authoritarian		0.067	0.156	-0.063	0.069
Participative			**0.407	**0.511	**0.374
Bureaucratic				**0.563	**0.308
Task-orientation					**0.495
Nurturant					

Source: Compiled from field survey

Table 10 presents the inter-correlations among leadership styles of Lower Level Executives of CBB. The 'participative' style was correlated significantly and positively with 'bureaucratic' style(r=0.407, P<0.01) 'task-orientation' style(r=0.511, P<0.01) and with 'nurturant' style(r=0.374, P<0.01) indicating that 'bureaucratic', 'task-orientation' and 'nurturant' styles increases with the higher level of 'participative' style.

The 'bureaucratic' style was correlated significantly and positively with 'task-orientation' style(r=0.563, P<0.01) and with 'nurturant' style(r=0.308, P<0.01) indicating that 'task-orientation' and 'nurturant' styles increases with the increase of 'bureaucratic' style.

The 'task-orientation' style was correlated significantly and positively with 'nurturant' style(r=0.495, P<0.01) indicating that 'nurturant' style increases with the increase of 'task-orientation' style. Hence, the hypothesis, thatthere is no significant relationship among leadership styles of employees of CBB is rejected in the case of 'participative' vs 'bureaucratic', 'participative' vs 'task-orientation', 'participative' vs 'nurturant', 'bureaucratic' vs 'task-orientation', 'bureaucratic' vs 'nurturant' and 'task-orientation' vs 'nurturant' and is accepted in all other cases.

Comparison of Lower Level Executives of LIC and CBB

In Lower Level Executives of LIC, 'authoritarian' style was significantly and positively correlated with 'task-orientation' and 'nurturant' styles whereas in Lower Level Executives of CBB, 'authoritarian' style does not correlate significantly with any other leadership style. In Lower Level Executives of LIC, 'participative' style was significantly and positively correlated with 'task-orientation' and 'nurturant' styles whereas in Lower Level Executives of CBB, 'participative' style was significantly and positively correlated with 'bureaucratic', 'task-orientation' and 'nurturant' styles. In Lower Level Executives of LIC, 'bureaucratic' style does not correlate significantly with any leadership style whereas in Lower Level Executives of CBB, 'bureaucratic' style was significantly and positively correlated with 'task-orientation' and 'nurturant' styles. In Lower Level Executives of LIC and CBB, 'task-orientation' style was significantly and positively correlated with 'nurturant' style.

Table 11 presents the inter-correlations among leadership styles of Clerks of LIC. The 'authoritarian' style was correlated significantly and positively with 'participative' style(r=0.152, P<0.05) and with 'nurturant' style(r=0.197, P<0.05) indicating that 'participative' and 'nurturant' styles increases with the higher role of 'authoritarian' style.

style was correlated significantly and positively with 'task-orientation' style(r=0.324, P<0.05) and with 'nurturant' style(r=0.598, P<0.01) indicating that 'task-orientation' and 'nurturant' styles increases with the higher level of 'authoritarian' style.

The 'participative' style was correlated significantly and positively with 'task-orientation' style(r=0.887, P<0.01) and with 'nurturant' style(r=0.629, P<0.01) indicating that 'task-orientation' and 'nurturant' styles increases with the increase of 'participative' style.

The 'task-orientation' style was correlated significantly and positively with 'nurturant' style(r=0.662, P<0.01) indicating that 'nurturant' styles increases with the increase of 'task-orientation' style. Hence, the hypothesis, that there is no significant relationship among leadership styles of employees of LIC is rejected in the case of 'authoritarian' vs 'task-orientation', 'authoritarian' vs 'nurturant', 'participative' vs 'task-orientation', 'participative' vs 'nurturant', and 'task-orientation' vs 'nurturant' and is accepted in all other cases.

Table 10
Inter-correlation of Leadership Styles for Lower Level Executives of CBB (N=107)

Leadership Styles	*Authoritarian*	*Participative*	*Bureaucratic*	*Task orientation*	*Nurturant*
Authoritarian		0.067	0.156	-0.063	0.069
Participative			**0.407	**0.511	**0.374
Bureaucratic				**0.563	**0.308
Task-orientation					**0.495
Nurturant					

Source: Compiled from field survey

Table 10 presents the inter-correlations among leadership styles of Lower Level Executives of CBB. The 'participative' style was correlated significantly and positively with 'bureaucratic' style(r=0.407, P<0.01) 'task-orientation' style(r=0.511, P<0.01) and with 'nurturant' style(r=0.374, P<0.01) indicating that 'bureaucratic', 'task-orientation' and 'nurturant' styles increases with the higher level of 'participative' style.

The 'bureaucratic' style was correlated significantly and positively with 'task-orientation' style($r=0.563$, $P<0.01$) and with 'nurturant' style($r=0.308$, $P<0.01$) indicating that 'task-orientation' and 'nurturant' styles increases with the increase of 'bureaucratic' style.

The 'task-orientation' style was correlated significantly and positively with 'nurturant' style($r=0.495$, $P<0.01$) indicating that 'nurturant' style increases with the increase of 'task-orientation' style. Hence, the hypothesis, thatthere is no significant relationship among leadership styles of employees of CBB is rejected in the case of 'participative' vs 'bureaucratic', 'participative' vs 'task-orientation', 'participative' vs 'nurturant', 'bureaucratic' vs 'task-orientation', 'bureaucratic' vs 'nurturant' and 'task-orientation' vs 'nurturant' and is accepted in all other cases.

Comparison of Lower Level Executives of LIC and CBB

In Lower Level Executives of LIC, 'authoritarian' style was significantly and positively correlated with 'task-orientation' and 'nurturant' styles whereas in Lower Level Executives of CBB, 'authoritarian' style does not correlate significantly with any other leadership style. In Lower Level Executives of LIC, 'participative' style was significantly and positively correlated with 'task-orientation' and 'nurturant' styles whereas in Lower Level Executives of CBB, 'participative' style was significantly and positively correlated with 'bureaucratic', 'task-orientation' and 'nurturant' styles. In Lower Level Executives of LIC, 'bureaucratic' style does not correlate significantly with any leadership style whereas in Lower Level Executives of CBB, 'bureaucratic' style was significantly and positively correlated with 'task-orientation' and 'nurturant' styles. In Lower Level Executives of LIC and CBB, 'task-orientation' style was significantly and positively correlated with 'nurturant' style.

Table 11 presents the inter-correlations among leadership styles of Clerks of LIC. The 'authoritarian' style was correlated significantly and positively with 'participative' style($r=0.152$, $P<0.05$) and with 'nurturant' style($r=0.197$, $P<0.05$) indicating that 'participative' and 'nurturant' styles increases with the higher role of 'authoritarian' style.

The 'participative' style was correlated significantly and positively with 'bureaucratic' style(r=0.563, P<0.01), 'task-orientation' style(r=0.779, P<0.01) and with 'nurturant' style(r=0.733, P<0.01) indicating that 'bureaucratic', 'task-orientation' and 'nurturant' styles increases with the increase of 'participative' style.

Table 11
Inter-correlation of Leadership Styles for Clerks of LIC (N=202)

Leadership Styles	*Authoritarian*	*Participative*	*Bureaucratic*	*Task orientation*	*Nurturant*
Authoritarian		*0.152	0.039	0.137	*0.197
Participative			**0.563	**0.779	**0.733
Bureaucratic				**0.533	**0.552
Task-orientation					**0.718
Nurturant					

Source: Compiled from field survey

The 'bureaucratic' style was correlated significantly and positively with 'task-orientation' style(r=0.533, P<0.01) and with 'nurturant' style(r=0.552, P<0.01) indicating that 'task-orientation' and 'nurturant' styles increases with the increase of 'bureaucratic' style.

Table 12
Inter-correlation of Leadership Styles for Clerks of CBB (N=329)

Leadership Styles	*Authoritarian*	*Participative*	*Bureaucratic*	*Task orientation*	*Nurturant*
Authoritarian		**0.373	**0.389	**0.375	**0.238
Participative			**0.564	**0.765	**0.713
Bureaucratic				**0.661	**0.586
Task-orientation					**0.749
Nurturant					

Source: Compiled from field survey

The 'task-orientation' style was correlated significantly and positively with 'nurturant' style(r=0.718, P<0.01) indicating that 'nurturant' styles increases with the increase of 'task-orientation' style. Hence, the hypothesis, that there is no significant relationship among leadership styles of employees of LIC is rejected in the case of 'authoritarian' vs 'participative', 'authoritarian' vs 'nurturant', 'participative vs 'bureaucratic', 'participative' vs 'task-orientation', 'participative' vs 'nurturant', 'bureaucratic' vs 'task-orientation', 'bureaucratic' vs 'nurturant', and 'task-orientation' vs 'nurturant' and is accepted in all other cases.

Table 12 presents the inter-correlations among leadership styles of clerks of CBB. All the leadership styles were correlated significantly and positively with all the other leadership styles. Hence, the hypothesis, that there is no significant relationship among leadership styles of employees of CBB is rejected.

Comparison of Clerks of LIC and CBB

In Clerks of LIC, 'authoritarian' style was significantly and positively correlated with 'participative' and 'nurturant' styles whereas in Clerks of CBB, 'authoritarian' style was significantly and positively correlated with 'participative', 'bureaucratic', 'task-orientation' and 'nurturant' styles. In Clerks of LIC and CBB, 'participative' style was significantly and positively correlated with 'bureaucratic', 'task-orientation' and 'nurturant' style. In Clerks of LIC and CBB, 'bureaucratic' style was significantly and positively correlated with 'task-orientation' and 'nurturant' style. In Clerks of LIC and CBB, 'task-orientation' style was significantly and positively correlated with 'nurturant' style.

6

THE DIFFERENCES OF LEADERSHIP STYLES IN INSURANCE AND BANKING SECTOR

INTRODUCTION

In order to know the difference of the leadership styles among the employees in CBB and LIC, the data is interpreted and presented in the following paragraphs:

The objectives of the study is to find out-

1 The difference of leadership styles at inter levels of employees of LIC about their self perception;
2 The difference of leadership styles at inter levels of employees of LIC as perceived by their subordinates;
3 The difference between leadership styles as judged by leader himself and as judged by his subordinates at different levels of employees of LIC.
4 The difference of leadership styles at inter levels of employees of CBB about their self perception;
5 The difference of leadership styles at inter levels of employees of CBB as perceived by their subordinates;
6 The difference between leadership styles as judged by leader himself and as judged by his subordinates at different levels of employees of CBB;
7 The difference of leadership styles at inter levels of employees of LIC and CBB about their self perception; and

8 The difference of leadership styles at inter levels of employees of LIC and CBB as perceived by their subordinates;

The data pertain to know the following findings.

(i) The difference between the leadership styles at inter levels of employees viz., Higher Level Executives and Middle Level Executives, Middle Level Executives and Lower Level Executives of LIC in self perception about their styles.

(ii) The difference between the leadership styles at inter levels of employees viz., Higher Level Executives and Middle Level Executives, Middle Level Executives and Lower Level Executives of LIC as perceived by their subordinates about their styles.

(iii) The difference between the leadership styles as judged by the leader himself and as judged by his immediate subordinates of different levels of employees viz., Higher Level Executives, Middle Level Executives and Lower Level Executives of LIC.

(iv) The difference between the leadership styles at inter levels of employees viz., Higher Level Executives and Middle Level Executives, Middle Level Executives and Lower Level Executives of CBB in self perception about their styles.

(v) The difference between the leadership styles at inter levels of employees viz., Higher Level Executives and Middle Level Executives, Middle Level Executives and Lower Level Executives of CBB as perceived by their subordinates about their styles.

(vi) The difference between the leadership styles as judged by the leader himself and as judged by his immediate subordinates of different levels of employees viz., Higher Level Executives, Middle Level Executives and Lower Level Executives of LIC.

(vii) The difference between the leadership styles at inter levels of employees viz., Higher Level Executives, Middle Level Executives and Lower Level Executives of LIC and CBB in self perception about their styles.

(viii) The difference between the leadership styles at inter levels of employees viz., Higher Level Executives, Middle Level Executives and Lower Level Executives of LIC and CBB as perceived by their subordinates about their styles.

THE DIFFERENCE BETWEEN LEADERSHIP STYLES OF EMPLOYEES OF LIC IN SELF PERCEPTION ABOUT THEIR STYLES

The leader's self perception reveals about the leadership styles of Higher Level Executives, Middle Level Executives and Lower Level Executives of LIC.

Scores on five leadership styles viz., authoritarian, participative, bureaucratic, task-orientation and nurturant were computed from leader's evaluation of ones own style.

With a view to find out difference between the two pairs viz., Higher Level Executives and Middle Level Executives; and Middle Level Executives and Lower Level Executives of LIC in self-perception about their leadership styles, mean, standard deviation were computed. Further, with an intent to find out significant difference between the five pairs 't' test was computed.

The difference between leadership styles of Higher Level Executives and Middle Level Executives of LIC in self perception about their styles

Table 1 presents mean, standard deviation and 't' values of the leadership styles as perceived by leaders themselves Higher Level Executives and Middle Level Executives of LIC.

Mean values of authoritarian, bureaucratic and nurturant styles are higher in Higher Level Executives than Middle Level Executives whereas mean values of participative and task-orientation styles are higher in Middle Level Executives than Higher Level Executives. In authoritarian, participative, task-orientation and nurturant styles, the Higher Level Executives and the Middle Level Executives do not differ significantly as the 't' values of these styles are less than the critical value (1.538, P<0.05; P0.145, P<0.05; To. 186; P<0.05 and N0.175, P<0.05). In bureaucratic style, the higher and middle level executives differ significantly as the 't' value is greater than the critical value (32.866, P<0.01). Hence, the hypothesis, that there is no significant difference among different leadership styles in the inter levels of employees of LIC in self perception about their styles" is rejected in the cae of bureaucratic style and is accepted in all other cases.

Table 1

Mean, Standard Deviation and 't' values of Leadership Styles of Higher Level Executives and Middle Level Executives of LIC as perceived by themselves

Leadership Styles	*Higher Level*			*Middle Level*			*'t' value*
	Mean	*N*	*S.D.*	*Mean*	*N*	*S.D*	
Authoritarian (A)	22.444	9	4.773	19.878	49	3.522	1.538
Participative (P)	24.111	9	1.269	24.204	49	3.391	0.145
Bureaucratic (B)	26.667	9	2.784	23.265	49	5.179	2.866
Task-orien tation (T)	25.778	9	3.420	26.000	49	2.492	0.186
Nurturant (N)	25.556	9	3.321	25.347	49	3.212	0.175

Source: Compiled from field survey

For 't' value, the degree of freedom (df) is N_1+N_2-2. In LIC, Higher Level Executives stood 9 where $N_1=9$, Middle Level Executives stood 49, where $N_2=49$, the df=N_1+N_2-2=>9+49-2=56. For 56 df the entries at 0.01 and 0.05 by linear interpolation are 2.704 and 2.021. The 't' values with two stars are significant at 0.01 level and those with one star at 0.05 level.

The difference between leadership styles of Middle Level Executives and Lower Level Executives of LIC in self perception about their styles

Table 2 presents mean, standard deviation and 't' values of the leadership styles as perceived by leaders themselves of Middle Level Executives and Lower Level Executives of LIC. Mean value of bureaucratic style is higher in Middle Level Executives than Lower Level Executives whereas mean values of authoritarian, participative, task-orientation and nurturant styles are higher in Lower Level Executives than Middle Level

Executives. In authoritarian, participative, bureaucratic and task-orientation styles, the Middle Level Executives and Lower Level Executives do not differ significantly as the 't' values of these styles are less than the critical value (1.423, P<0.05; P1.823, P<0.05; B0.016, P<0.05; T0.625, P<0.05). In Nurturant style, the middle and lower level executives differ significantly as the 't' value is greater than the critical value (N3.491, P<0.01). Hence, the hypothesis, that there is no significant difference among different leadership styles in the inter levels of employees of LIC in self perception about their styles" is rejected in the case of nurturant style and is accepted in all other cases.

Table 2

Mean, Standard Deviation and 't' values of Leadership Styles of Middle Level Executives and Lower Level Executives of LIC as perceived by themselves

Leadership Styles	*Middle Level*			*Lower Level*			*'t' value*
	Mean	*N*	*S.D.*	*Mean*	*N*	*S.D*	
Authoritarian (A)	19.878	49	3.522	21.200	40	4.937	1.423
Participative (P)	24.204	49	3.391	25.575	40	3.637	1.823
Bureaucratic (B)	23.265	49	5.179	23.250	40	3.888	0.016
Task-orien tation (T)	26.000	49	2.492	26.325	40	2.401	0.625
Nurturant (N)	25.347	49	3.212	27.375	40	2.250	3.491

Source: Compiled from field survey

For 't' value, the degree of freedom (df) is N_1+N_2-2. In LIC, Middle Level Executives stood 49 where $N_1=49$, Lower Level Executives stood 40, where $N_2=40$, the df=N_1+N_2-2=>49+40-2=87. For 87 df the entries at 0.01 and 0.05 by linear interpolation are 2.660 and 2.000. The 't' values with two stars are significant at 0.01 level and those with one star at 0.05 level.

THE DIFFERENCE BETWEEN LEADERSHIP STYLES OF EMPLOYEES OF LIC AS PERCEIVED BY THEIR SUBORDINATES

The subordinates' perception on superior styles reveals about the leadership styles of Higher Level Executives, Middle Level Executives and Lower Level Executives of LIC.

Scores on five leadership styles viz., authoritarian, participative, bureaucratic, task-orientation and nurturant were computed from subordinates perception on superior styles.

With a view to find out difference between the five pairs viz., Higher Level Executives and Middle Level Executives; and Middle Level Executives and Lower Level Executives of LIC as perceived by their subordinates about their leadership styles, mean, standard deviation were computed. Further, with an intent to find out significant difference between the five pairs 't' test was computed.

The difference between leadership styles of Higher Level Executives and Middle Level Executives of LIC as perceived by their subordinates.

Table 3 presents mean, standard deviation and 't' values of the leadership styles as perceived by their subordinates Higher Level Executives and Middle Level Executives of LIC. Mean values of authoritative and nurturant styles are higher in Higher Level Executives than Middle Level Executives whereas mean value of participative, task-orientation styles are higher in Middle Level Executives than Higher Level Executives. In authoritarian, participative, bureaucratic, task-orientation and nurturant styles, the Higher Level Executives and the Middle Level Executives do not differ significantly as the 't' values of

Table 3
Mean, Standard Deviation and 't' values of Leadership Styles of Higher Level Executives and Middle Level Executives of LIC as perceived by their subordinates

Leadership Styles	*Higher Level*			*Middle Level*			*'t' value*
	Mean	*N*	*S.D.*	*Mean*	*N*	*S.D*	
Authoritarian (A)	17.204	49	4.449	16.050	40	5.063	1.129
Participative (P)	22.204	49	3.247	23.025	40	4.172	1.019
Bureaucratic (B)	22.082	49	3.829	26.000	40	2.792	5.573
Task-orien tation (T)	23.673	49	3.112	24.150	40	3.512	0.671
Nurturant (N)	23.673	49	3.986	23.325	40	4.002	0.409

Source: Compiled from field survey

these styles are less than the critical value (A1.129, P<0.05; P1.019, P<0.05; T0.671, P<0.05 and N0.409, P<0.05). In bureaucratic style, the higher and middle level executives differ significantly as the 't' value is greater than the critical value (B5.573, P<0.01). Hence, the hypothesis, that "there is no significant difference among different leadership styles in the inter levels of employees of LIC as perceived by their subordinates" is rejected in the case of bureaucratic style and is accepted in all other cases.

For 't' value, the degree of freedom (df) is N_1+N_2-2. In LIC, Higher Level Executives subordinates stood 49 where $N_1=49$, Middle Level Executives subordinates stood 40, where $N_2=40$, the df=N_1+N_2-2=>49+40-2=87. For 87 df the entries at 0.01 and 0.05 by linear interpolation are 2.660 and 2.000. The 't' values with two stars are significant at 0.01 level and those with one star at 0.05 level.

The difference between leadership styles of Middle Level Executives and Lower Level Executives of LIC as perceived by their subordinates.

Table 4 presents mean, standard deviation and 't' values of the leadership styles as perceived by their subordinates of Middle Level Executives and Lower Level Executives of LIC. Mean values of participative, bureaucratic, task-orientation and nurturant styles are higher in Middle Level Executives

Table 4

Mean, Standard Deviation and 't' values of Leadership Styles of Middle Level Executives and Lower Level Executives of LIC as perceived by subordinates

Leadership Styles	*Middle Level*			*Lower Level*			*'t' value*
	Mean	*N*	*S.D.*	*Mean*	*N*	*S.D*	
Authoritarian (A)	16.050	40	5.063	18.030	202	4.361	2.31
Participative (P)	23.025	40	4.172	22.520	202	3.923	0.706
Bureaucratic (B)	26.000	40	2.792	23.426	202	4.423	4.767
Task-orien tation (T)	24.150	40	3.512	23.020	202	3.007	2.089
Nurturant (N)	23.325	40	4.002	23.257	202	3.08	0.102

Source: Compiled from field survey

than Lower Level Executives whereas mean value of authoritative style is higher in Lower Level Executives than Middle Level Executives. In participative and nurturant styles, the Middle Level Executives and Lower Level Executives of LIC do not differ significantly as the 't' values of these styles are less than the critical value (P0.706, P<0.05; and N0.102, P<0.05). In authoritarian, bureaucratic and Task-orientation styles, the middle and lower level executives differ significantly as the 't' values are greater than the critical value. (A2.31, P<001, B4.767, P<0.01 and T2.089, P<0.05). Hence, the hypothesis, that there is no significant difference among different leadership styles in the inter levels of employees in LIC as perceived by their subordinates is accepted in the case of participative and nurturant styles and is rejected in all other cases.

For 't' value, the degree of freedom (df) is N_1+N_2-2. In LIC Middle Level Executives subordinates stood 40 where $N_1=40$, Lower Level Executives subordinates stood 202, where $N_2=202$, the $df=N_1+N_2-2 => 40+202-2=240$. For 240 df the entries at 0.01 and 0.05 by linear interpolation are 2.576 and 1.960. The 't' values with two stars are significant at 0.01 level and those with one star at 0.05 level.

THE DIFFERENCE BETWEEN LEADERSHIP STYLES AS JUDGED BY LEADER HIMSELF AND AS JUDGED BY HIS SUBORDINATES' OF DIFFERENT LEVELS OF EMPLOYEES OF LIC

The leader's self perception and the subordinates' perception on superior styles reveals about the leadership styles of Higher Level Executives, Middle Level Executives and Lower Level Executives of LIC.

Scores on five leadership styles viz., authoritarian, participative, bureaucratic, task-orientation and nurturant were computed from both leader's evaluation of ones own style and subordinates perception on superior's styles.

With a view to find out difference between leadership style of a superior, as judged by the superior himself and as judged by his immediate subordinates, the analysis was done at three levels viz., Higher Level Executives, Middle Level Executives and Lower Level Executives. Firstly, for the Higher Level Executives level the leader self perception scores were juxtaposed with the average score on subordinates (Middle Level Executives) perception on superior style. Secondly, for the Middle Level Executives level the leader self perception scores were juxtaposed with the average score on subordinates (Lower Level Executives) perception on superior style. Thirdly, for the Lower Level Executives level the leader self perception scores were juxtaposed with the average score on subordinates (Clerks) perception on superior style. For all this 't' test was used to find out the significant difference between the leaders self perception and as perceived by their subordinates.

The difference between leadership styles of Higher Level Executives self perception and as perceived by their subordinates of LIC

Table 5 presents the difference between leadership styles as judged by the leader himself and as judged by his immediate subordinates of Higher Level Executives of LIC. Mean values of authoritarian, participative, bureaucratic, task-orientation and nurturant styles are higher in self judgement of Higher Level Executives than judged by his subordinates. In task-orientation and nurturant styles of the Higher Level Executives self judgement and as judged by his immediate subordinates do not differ significantly as the 't' values of these styles are less than the critical value (T0.115, $P<0.05$ and N0.124, $P<0.05$). In authoritarian, participative and bureaucratic styles, higher level executives in self judgement and as judged by subordinates differ significantly as the 't' values are greater than the critical value (A3.059, $P<0.01$; P 3.037, $P<0.01$ and B4.257, $P<0.01$). Hence, the hypothesis, that there is no significant difference in leadership styles of employees of LIC as judged by leader himself and as judged by his subordinates is accepted in the cae of Task-orientation and nurturant styles and is rejected in all other cases.

Table 5
Mean, Standard Deviation and 't' values for five Leadership Styles of Higher Level Executives as judged by leader himself and as judged by his subordinates of LIC

Leadership Styles	*Self Judgement*			*Judged by his subordinates*			*'t' value*
	Mean	*N*	*S.D.*	*Mean*	*N*	*S.D*	
Authoritarian (A)	22.444	9	4.773	17.204	49	4.449	3.054
Participative (P)	24.111	9	1.269	22.204	49	3.247	3.037
Bureaucratic (B)	26.667	9	2.784	22.082	49	3.829	4.257
Task-orien tation (T)	25.778	9	3.420	23.673	49	3.112	1.720
Nurturant (N)	25.556	9	3.321	23.673	49	3.986	1.512

Source: Compiled from field survey

For 't' value, the degree of freedom (df) is N_1+N_2-2. In LIC, Higher Level Executives stood 9 where $N_1=9$, Higher Level Executives subordinates stood 49, where $N_2=49$, the df=N_1+N_2-2=>9+49-2=57. For 57 df the entries at 0.01 and 0.05 by linear interpolation are 2.704 and 2.021. The 't' values with two stars are significant at 0.01 level and those with one star at 0.05 level.

The difference between leadership styles of Middle Level Executives self perception and as perceived by their subordinates of LIC

Table 6 presents the difference between leadership styles as judged by the leader himself and as judged by his immediate subordinates of Middle Level Executives of LIC. Mean values of authoritarian, participative, task-orientation and nurturant styles are higher in self judgement of Middle Level Executives than judged by his subordinates whereas mean values of bureaucratic style is higher in judged by Middle Level Executives subordinates than self judgement. In authoritarian, bureaucratic, task-orientation and nurturant styles of the Middle Level Executives self judgement and as judged by his immediate subordinates differ significantly as the 't' values of these styles are greater than the critical value (A4.038, $P<0.05$; B3.173, $P<0.05$; T2.803, $P<0.05$ and N2.586, $P<0.05$).

In participative style, the middle level executives in self judgement and as judged by subordinates do not differ significantly as the 't' values is lessthan the critical value (P1.441, $P<0.05$). Hence, the hypothesis, there is no significant difference in leadership styles of employees of LIC as judged by leader himself and as judged by his subordinates is accepted in the case of participative style and is rejected in all other cases..

Table 6

Mean, Standard Deviation and 't' values for five Leadership Styles of Middle Level Executives as judged by leader himself and as judged by his subordinates of LIC

Leadership Styles	*Self Judgement*			*Judged by his subordinates*			*'t' value*
	Mean	*N*	*S.D.*	*Mean*	*N*	*S.D*	
Authoritarian (A)	19.878	49	3.522	16.05	40	5.063	4.038
Participative (P)	24.204	49	3.391	23.025	40	4.172	1.441
Bureaucratic (B)	23.265	49	5.179	26.00	40	2.792	3.173
Task-orien tation (T)	26.000	49	2.492	24.15	40	3.512	2.803
Nurturant (N)	25.347	49	3.212	23.325	40	4.002	2.586

Source: Compiled from field survey

For 't' value, the degree of freedom (df) is N_1+N_2-2. In LIC, Middle Level Executives stood 49 where $N_1=49$, Middle Level Executivess subordinates stood 40, where $N_2=40$, the $df=N_1+N_2-2=>49+40-2=87$. For 87 df the entries at 0.01 and 0.05 by linear interpolation are 2.660 and 2.000. The 't' values with two stars are significant at 0.01 level and those with one star at 0.05 level.

The difference between leadership styles of Lower Level Executives self perception and as perceived by their subordinates of LIC

Table 7 presents the difference between leadership styles as judged by the leader himself and as judged by his immediate subordinates of Lower Level Executives of LIC. Mean values of authoritarian, participative, task-orientation and nurturant styles are higher in self judgement of Lower Level Executives

Table 7
Mean, Standard Deviation and 't' values for five Leadership Styles of Lower Level Executives as judged by leader himself and as judged by his subordinates of LIC

Leadership Styles	*Self Judgement*			*Judged by his subordinates*			*'t' value*
	Mean	*N*	*S.D.*	*Mean*	*N*	*S.D*	
Authoritarian (A)	21.200	40	4.937	18.03	202	4.361	3.778
Participative (P)	25.575	40	3.637	22.520	202	3.923	4.781
Bureaucratic (B)	23.250	40	3.888	23.426	202	4.423	0.255
Task-orien tation (T)	26.325	40	2.401	23.020	202	3.007	7.598
Nurturant (N)	27.375	40	2.250	23.257	202	3.080	9.875

Source: Compiled from field survey

than judged by his subordinates whereas Mean Values of bureaucratic style is higher in judged by his subordinates than the lower level executives. In authoritarian, participative, task-orientation and nurturant styles of the Lower Level Executives self judgement and as judged by his immediate subordinates differ significantly as the 't' values of these styles are greater than the critical value (A3.778,P<0.05; P4.781, P<0.05; T7.598, P<0.05 and N9.875, P<0.05). In bureaucratic style, the lower level executives in self judgement and as judged by subordinates do not differ significantly as the 't' values is less than the critical value (B0.255, P>0.05). Hence, the hypothesis, that there is no significant difference in leadership styles of employees of LIC as judged by leader himself and as judged by his subordinates is accepted in the case of bureaucratic style and is rejected in all other cases.

For 't' value, the degree of freedom (df) is N_1+N_2-2. In LIC, Lower Level Executives stood 40 where $N_1=40$, Lower Level Executivess subordinates stood 202, where $N_2=202$, the df=N_1+N_2-2=>40+202-2=240. For 240 df the entries at 0.01 and 0.05 by linear interpolation are 2.576 and 1.960. The 't' values with two stars are significant at 0.01 level and those with one star at 0.05 level.

THE DIFFERENCE BETWEEN LEADERSHIP STYLES OF EMPLOYEES OF CBB IN SELF PERCEPTION ABOUT THEIR STYLES

The difference between leadership styles of Higher Level Executives and Middle Level Executives of CBB in self perception about their styles.

Table 8

Mean, Standard Deviation and 't' values of Leadership Styles of Higher Level Executives and Middle Level Executives of CBB as perceived by themselves

Leadership Styles	*Higher Level Executives*			*Middle Level Executives*			*'t' value*
	Mean	*N*	*S.D.*	*Mean*	*N*	*S.D*	
Authoritarian (A)	21.267	30	5.496	19.235	34	4.031	0.667
Participative (P)	26.467	30	3.071	25.824	34	2.645	0.892
Bureaucratic (B)	25.100	30	3.100	23.559	34	4.906	1.52
Task-orien tation (T)	26.800	30	2.024	25.088	34	1.975	3.417
Nurturant (N)	26.600	30	4.005	25.471	34	2.620	1.532

Source: Compiled from field survey

Table 8 presents mean, standard deviation and 't' values of the leadership styles as perceived by leaders themselves Higher Level Executives and Middle Level Executives of CBB. Mean values of authoritarian, participative, bureaucratic, and nurturant styles are higher in Higher Level Executives than Middle Level Executives. In authoritarian, participative, bureaucratic, task-orientation and nurturant styles, the Higher Level Executives and the Middle Level Executives do not differ significantly as the 't' values of these styles are less than the critical value (A1.667, $P<0.05$; P0.892, $P<0.05$; B1.52, $P<0.05$; and N1.532, $P<0.05$). In task-orientation style, the higher and middle level executives differ significantly as the 't' values are greater than the critical value (T3.417, $P<0.01$). Hence, the hypothesis, that there is no significant difference among different leadership styles in the inter levels of employees of CBB in self perception about their styles is accepted in the case of task-orientation style and is rejected in all other cases.

For 't' value, the degree of freedom (df) is N_1+N_2-2. In CBB, Higher Level Executives stood 30 where $N_1=30$, Middle

Level Executives stood 34, where N_2=34, the df=N_1+N_2-2=>30+34-2=62. For 62 df the entries at 0.01 and 0.05 by linear interpolation are 2.660 and 2.000. The 't' values with two stars are significant at 0.01 level and those with one star at 0.05 level.

The difference between leadership styles of Middle Level Executives and Lower Level Executives of CBB in self perception about their styles

Table 9 presents mean, standard deviation and 't' values of the leadership styles as perceived by leaders themselves of Middle Level Executives and Lower Level Executives of CBB. Mean values of participative and task-orientation styles are higher in Middle Level Executives than Lower Level Executives

Table 9
Mean, Standard Deviation and 't' values of Leadership Styles of Middle Level Executives and Lower Level Executives of CBB as perceived by themselves

Leadership Styles	*Middle Level*			*Lower Level*			*'t' value*
	Mean	*N*	*S.D.*	*Mean*	*N*	*S.D*	
Authoritarian (A)	19.235	34	4.031	20.916	107	4.398	2.07
Participative (P)	25.824	34	2.645	25.458	107	2.593	0.707
Bureaucratic (B)	23.559	34	4.906	23.748	107	4.402	0.2
Task-orien tation (T)	25.088	34	1.975	25.056	107	2.306	0.079
Nurturant (N)	25.471	34	2.620	26.308	107	2.860	1.585

Source: Compiled from field survey

whereas mean values of authoritarian, bureaucratic and nurturant styles are higher in Lower Level Executives than Middle Level Executives. In participative, bureaucratic, task-orientation and nurturant styles, the Middle Level Executives and Lower Level Executives do not differ significantly as the 't' values of these styles are less than the critical value (P0.707, P<0.05; B0.2, P<0.05; T0.079, P<0.05 and N1.585, P<0.05). In authoritarian style, the middle and lower level executive differ significantly as the 't' values are greater than the critical value (A2.07, P0.05). Hence, the hypothesis, that there is no significant difference among different leadership styles in the inter levels

of employees of CBB in self perception about their styles is accepted in the case of authoritarian style and in rejected in all other cases.

For 't' value, the degree of freedom (df) is N_1+N_2-2. In CBB, Middle Level Executives stood 34 where $N_1=34$, Lower Level Executives stood 107, where $N_2=107$, the $df=N_1+N_2-2$=>34+107-2=139. For 139 df the entries at 0.01 and 0.05 by linear interpolation are 2.576 and 1.960. The 't' values with two stars are significant at 0.01 level and those with one star at 0.05 level.

THE DIFFERENCE BETWEEN LEADERSHIP STYLES OF EMPLOYEES OF CBB AS PERCEIVED BY THEIR SUBORDINATES

The difference between leadership styles of Higher Level Executives and Middle Level Executives of CBB as perceived by their subordinates

Table 10 presents mean, standard deviation and 't' values of the leadership styles as perceived by their subordinates Higher Level Executives and Middle Level Executives of CBB. Mean values of authoritarian, participative, bureaucratic, task-orientation and nurturant styles are higher in Middle Level Executives than Higher Level Executives. In participative and bureaucratic styles, the Higher Level Executives and the Middle Level Executives do not differ significantly as the 't' values of these styles are less than the critical value (P1.725,

Table 10
Mean, Standard Deviation and 't' values of Leadership Styles of Higher Level Executives and Middle Level Executives of CBB as perceived by their subordinates

Leadership Styles	*Higher Level*			*Middle Level*			*'t' value*
	Mean	*N*	*S.D.*	*Mean*	*N*	*S.D*	
Authoritarian (A)	21.529	34	4.336	21.841	107	5.448	0.342
Participative (P)	22.029	34	4.489	23.495	107	3.730	1.725
Bureaucratic (B)	21.706	34	4.462	23.047	107	3.820	1.578
Task-orien tation (T)	21.941	34	4.735	24.673	107	2.818	3.188
Nurturant (N)	22.735	34	4.259	26.495	107	9.165	3.275

Source: Compiled from field survey

P<0.05; B1.578, P<0.05) In authoritarian, talk-oientation and nurturant style, the higher and middle level executives differ significantly as the 't' values are greater than the critical value (A3.42, P<0.01; T3.188, P<0.01 and N3.275, P<0.01). Hence, the hypothesis, that there is no significant difference among different leadership styles in the inter levels of employees of CBB as perceived by their subordinates is accepted in participatie and bureaucratic style and is rejected in all other cases.

For 't' value, the degree of freedom (df) is N_1+N_2-2. In CBB, Higher Level Executives subordinates stood 34 where $N_1=34$, Middle Level Executives subordinates stood 107, where $N_2=107$, the $df=N_1+N_2-2=>34+107-2=139$. For 139 df the entries at 0.01 and 0.05 by linear interpolation are 2.576 and 1.960. The 't' values with two stars are significant at 0.01 level and those with one star at 0.05 level.

The difference between leadership styles of Middle Level Executives and Lower Level Executives of CBB as perceived by their subordinates

Table 11 presents mean, standard deviation and 't' values of the leadership styles as perceived by their subordinates of Middle Level Executives and Lower Level Executives of CBB. Mean values of authoritative, participative, bureaucratic, task-orientation and nurturant styles are higher in Middle Level Executives than Lower Level Executives. In authoritarian,

Table 11
Mean, Standard Deviation and 't' values of Leadership Styles of Middle Level Executives and Lower Level Executives of CBB as perceived by subordinates

Leadership Styles	*Middle Level*			*Lower Level*			*'t' value*
	Mean	*N*	*S.D.*	*Mean*	*N*	*S.D*	
Authoritarian (A)	21.841	107	5.448	20.024	329	5.777	3.704
Participative (P)	23.495	107	3.73	22.444	329	4.59	4.646
Bureaucratic (B)	23.047	107	3.82	21.447	329	4.063	4.436
Task-orien tation (T)	24.673	107	2.818	23.033	329	4.078	2.95
Nurturant (N)	26.495	107	9.165	22.432	329	4.393	2.383

Source: Compiled from field survey

participative, bureaucratic, task-orientation and nurturant styles, the Middle Level Executives and Lower Level Executives of CBB differ significantly as the 't' values of these styles are greater than the critical value (A3.704, $P<0.05$; P4.646, $P<0.05$; B4.436, $P<0.05$; T2.95, $P<0.05$ and N7.383, $P<0.05$). Hence, the hypothesis, that there is no significant difference among different leadership styles in the inter levels of employees in CBB as perceived by their subordinates is rejected.

For 't' value, the degree of freedom (df) is N_1+N_2-2. In CBB, Middle Level Executives subordinates stood 107 where $N_1=107$, Lower Level Executives subordinates stood 329, where $N_2=329$, the df=N_1+N_2-2=>107+329-2=434. For 434 df the entries at 0.01 and 0.05 by linear interpolation are 2.576 and 1.960. The 't' values with two stars are significant at 0.01 level and those with one star at 0.05 level.

THE DIFFERENCE BETWEEN LEADERSHIP STYLES AS JUDGED BY LEADER HIMSELF AND AS JUDGED BY HIS SUBORDINATES OF DIFFERENT LEVELS OF EMPLOYEES OF CBB

The difference between leadership styles of Higher Level Executives self perception and as perceived by their subordinates of CBB

Table 12

Mean, Standard Deviation and 't' values for five Leadership Styles of Higher Level Executives as judged by leader himself and as judged by his subordinates of CBB

Leadership Styles	*Self Judgement*			*Judged by his subordinates*			*'t' value*
	Mean	*N*	*S.D.*	*Mean*	*N*	*S.D*	
Authoritarian (A)	21.267	30	5.496	21.529	34	4.336	0.21
Participative (P)	26.467	30	3.071	22.029	34	4.489	4.662
Bureaucratic (B)	25.100	30	3.100	21.706	34	4.462	3.565
Task-orien tation (T)	26.800	30	2.024	21.941	34	4.735	5.447
Nurturant (N)	26.600	30	4.005	22.735	34	4.259	3.738

Source: Compiled from field survey

Table 12 presents the difference between leadership styles as judged by the leader himself and as judged by his immediate

subordinates of Higher Level Executives of CBB. Mean values of participative, bureaucratic, task-orientation and nurturant styles are higher in self judgement of Higher Level Executives than judged by his subordinates whereas mean value of authoritarian style is higher in subordinates perception of Higher Level Executives than self judgement. In authoritarian, participative, bureaucratic, task-orientation and nurturant styles of the Higher Level Executives self judgement and as judged by his immediate subordinates differ significantly as the 't' values of these styles are greater than the critical value (P4.662, $P<0.05$; B3.565, $P<0.05$; T5.447, $P<0.05$ and N3.738, $P<0.05$). In authoritarian style, higher level executives in self judgement and as judged by subordinates do not differ significantly as the 't' value is less than the critical value (A0.21, $P<0.05$). Hence, the hypothesis, that there is no significant difference in leadership styles of employees of CBB as judged by leader himself and as judged by his subordinates is accepted in authoritarian style and is rejected in all other cases.

For 't' value, the degree of freedom (df) is N_1+N_2-2. In CBB, Higher Level Executives stood 30 where $N_1=30$, Higher Level Executives subordinates stood 34, where $N_2=34$, the df=N_1+N_2-2=>30+34-2=62. For 62 df the entries at 0.01 and 0.05 by linear interpolation are 2.660 and 2.000. The 't' values with two stars are significant at 0.01 level and those with one star at 0.05 level.

The difference between leadership styles of Middle Level Executives self perception and as perceived by their subordinates of CBB

Table 13 presents the difference between leadership styles as judged by the leader himself and as judged by his immediate subordinates of Middle Level Executives of CBB. Mean values of participative, bureaucratic and task-orientation styles are higher in self judgement of Middle Level Executives than judged by his subordinates whereas mean values of authoritarian and nurturant styles are higher in judged by Middle Level Executives subordinates than self judgement. In bureaucratic, task-orientation and nurturant styles of the

Middle Level Executives self judgement and as judged by his immediate subordinates do not differ significantly as the 't' values of these styles are less than the critical value (B0.557, P<0.05; T0.954, P<0.05 and N1.031, P<0.05). In authoritarian and participative style, middle level executives in self judgement and judged by subordinates differ significantly as the 't' values are greater than the critical value (A2.909, P<0.01; P4.023, P<0.01). Hence, the hypothesis, that there is no significant difference in leadership styles of employees of CBB as judged by leader himself and as judged by his subordinates is accepted in bureaucratic, task-orientation and nurturant style and rejectedin all othe cases.

Table 13
Mean, Standard Deviation and 't' values for five Leadership Styles of Middle Level Executives as judged by leader himself and as judged by his subordinates of CBB

Leadership Styles	*Self Judgement*			*Judged by his subordinates*			*'t' value*
	Mean	*N*	*S.D.*	*Mean*	*N*	*S.D*	
Authoritarian (A)	19.235	34	4.031	21.841	107	5.448	2.999
Participative (P)	25.824	34	2.645	23.495	107	3.73	4.023
Bureaucratic (B)	23.559	34	4.906	23.047	107	3.82	0.557
Task-orien tation (T)	25.088	34	1.975	24.673	107	2.818	0.954
Nurturant (N)	25.471	34	2.62	26.495	107	9.165	1.031

Source: Compiled from field survey

For 't' value, the degree of freedom (df) is N_1+N_2-2. In CBB, Middle Level Executives stood 34 where $N_1=34$, Middle Level Executivess subordinates stood 107, where $N_2=107$, the df=N_1+N_2-2=>34+107-2=139. For 139 df the entries at 0.01 and 0.05 by linear interpolation are 2.576 and 1.960. The 't' values with two stars are significant at 0.01 level and those with one star at 0.05 level.

The difference between leadership styles of Lower Level Executives self perception and as perceived by their subordinates of CBB

Table 14 presents the difference between leadership styles as judged by the leader himself and as judged by his immediate subordinates of Lower Level Executives of CBB. Mean values of authoritarian, participative, bureaucratic, task-orientation and nurturant styles are higher in self judgement of Lower Level Executives than judged by his subordinates. In participative, bureaucratic, task-orientation and nurturant styles of the Lower Level Executives self judgement and as judged by his immediate subordinates differ significantly as the 't' values of these styles are greater than the critical value (P8.466, P<0.05; B4.784, P<0.05; T20.23, P<0.05 and N10.553, P<0.05). In authoritarian style, lower level executives in self judgement and judged by subordinates do not differ significantly as the 't' value is less than the critical value (A1.68, P<0.05). Hence, the hypothesis, that there is no significant difference in leadership styles of employees of CBB as judged by leader himself and as judged by his subordinates is rejected in authoritarian style and is accepted in all other cases.

Table 14

Mean, Standard Deviation and 't' values for five Leadership Styles of Lower Level Executives as judged by leader himself and as judged by his subordinates of CBB

Leadership Styles	*Self Judgement*			*Judged by his subordinates*			*'t' value*
	Mean	*N*	*S.D.*	*Mean*	*N*	*S.D*	
Authoritarian (A)	20.916	107	4.398	20.024	329	5.777	1.68
Participative (P)	25.458	107	2.593	22.444	329	4.59	8.466
Bureaucratic (B)	23.748	107	4.402	21.447	329	4.063	4.784
Task-orien tation (T)	25.056	107	2.306	23.033	329	4.078	20.23
Nurturant (N)	26.308	107	2.860	22.432	329	4.393	10.533

Source: Compiled from field survey

For 't' value, the degree of freedom (df) is N_1+N_2-2. In CBB, Lower Level Executives stood 107 where $N_1=107$, Lower Level Executivess subordinates stood 329, where $N_2=329$, the $df=N_1+N_2-2=>107+329-2=434$. For 434 df the entries at 0.01 and 0.05 by linear interpolation are 2.576 and 1.960. The 't' values with two stars are significant at 0.01 level and those with one star at 0.05 level.

THE DIFFERENCE BETWEEN LEADERSHIP STYLES OF EMPLOYEES OF LIC AND CBB IN SELF PERCEPTION ABOUT THEIR STYLES

The difference of leadership styles of Higher Level Executives between LIC and CBB in self perception about their styles

Table 15 presents mean, standard deviation and 't' values of the leadership styles of Higher Level Executives of LIC and CBB as perceived by leaders themselves. Mean values of authoritarian and bureaucratic styles are higher in Higher Level Executives of LIC than Higher Level Executives of CBB whereas mean values of participative, nurturant and task-orientation styles are higher in Higher Level Executives of CBB than Higher Level Executives of LIC. In authoritarian, bureaucratic, task-orientation and nurturant styles, the Higher Level Executives of LIC and CBB do not differ significantly as the 't' values of these styles are less than the critical value (A0.626, $P<0.05$; B1.442, $P<0.05$; T0.853, $P<0.05$ and N0.787, $P<0.05$). In participative style, the higher level executives differ significantly as the 't' value is greater than the critical value (P3.356, $P<0.01$). Hence, the hypothesis, that there is no significant difference among different leadership styles of employees of LIC and CBB in self perception about their styles is rejected in participative style and is accepted in all other cases.

Table 15

Mean, Standard Deviation and 't' values of Leadership Styles of Higher Level Executives of LIC and CBB as perceived by themselves

Leadership Styles	*LIC Higher Level*			*CBB Higher Level*			*'t' value*
	Mean	*N*	*S.D.*	*Mean*	*N*	*S.D*	
Authoritarian (A)	22.444	9	4.773	21.267	30	5.496	0.626
Participative (P)	24.111	9	1.269	26.467	30	3.071	3.356
Bureaucratic (B)	26.667	9	2.784	25.100	30	3.100	1.442
Task-orien tation (T)	25.778	9	3.42	26.800	30	2.024	0.853
Nurturant (N)	25.556	9	3.321	26.600	30	4.005	0.787

Source: Compiled from field survey

For 't' value, the degree of freedom (df) is N_1+N_2-2. In LIC, Higher Level Executives stood 9 where $N_1=9$, in CBB Higher Level Executives stood 30, where $N_2=30$, the df=N_1+N_2-2=>9+30-2=37. For 37 df the entries at 0.01 and 0.05 by linear interpolation are 2.704 and 2.021. The 't' values with two stars are significant at 0.01 level and those with one star at 0.05 level.

The difference of leadership styles of Middle Level Executives between LIC and CBB in self perception about their styles

Table 16 presents mean, standard deviation and 't' values of the leadership styles of Middle Level Executives of LIC and CBB as perceived by leaders themselves. Mean values of authoritarian and task-orientation styles are higher in Middle Level Executives of LIC than Middle Level Executives of CBB whereas mean values of participative, bureaucratic, and nurturant styles are higher in Middle Level Executives of CBB than Middle Level Executives of LIC. In authoritarian, bureaucratic, task-orientation and nurturant styles, the Middle Level Executives of LIC and CBB do not differ significantly as the 't' values of these styles are less than the critical value (A0.455, P<0.05; B0.794, P<0.05; T0.067, P<0.05 and N0.848, P<0.05). In participative style, the middle level executives of LIC and CBB differ significantly at the 't' value is greater than the critical value (P2.44, P<0.01). Hence, the hypothesis, that there is no significant difference among different leadership styles of employees of LIC and CBB in self perception about

Table 16
Mean, Standard Deviation and 't' values of Leadership Styles of Middle Level Executives of LIC and CBB as perceived by themselves

Leadership Styles	*LIC Middle Level*			*CBB Middle Level*			*'t' value*
	Mean	*N*	*S.D.*	*Mean*	*N*	*S.D*	
Authoritarian (A)	19.878	49	3.522	19.235	34	4.031	0.752
Participative (P)	24.204	49	3.391	25.824	34	2.645	2.44
Bureaucratic (B)	23.265	49	5.179	23.559	34	4.906	0.263
Task-orien tation (T)	26.000	49	2.492	25.088	34	1.975	1.857
Nurturant (N)	25.347	49	3.212	25.471	34	2.620	0.193

Source: Compiled from field survey

their styles is rejected in participative style and as accepted in all other cases.

For 't' value, the degree of freedom (df) is N_1+N_2-2. In LIC, Middle Level Executives stood 49 where $N_1=49$, in CBB Middle Level Executives stood 34, where $N_2=34$, the df=N_1+N_2-2=>49+34-2=81. For 81 df the entries at 0.01 and 0.05 by linear interpolation are 2.660 and 2.000. The 't' values with two stars are significant at 0.01 level and those with one star at 0.05 level.

The difference of leadership styles of Lower Level Executives between LIC and CBB in self perception about their styles

Table 17 presents mean, standard deviation and 't' values of the leadership styles of Lower Level Executives of LIC and CBB as perceived by leaders themselves. Mean values of authoritarian, participative, task-orientation and nurturant styles are higher in Lower Level Executives of LIC than Lower Level Executives of CBB whereas mean value of bureaucratic style is higher in Lower Level Executives of CBB than Lower Level Executives of LIC. In authoritarian, participative, bureaucratic, task-orientation and nurturant styles, the Lower Level Executives of LIC and CBB do not differ significantly as the 't' values of these styles are less than the critical value (A0.32, $P<0.05$; P0.187, $P<0.05$; B0.666, $P<0.05$. In task-orientatin and nurturant styles, the lower level executives of LIC and CB differ significantly as the 't' value are greater than the critical value (T2.884, $P<0.01$ and N2.371, $P<0.01$). Hence, the hypothesis, that there is no significant difference among

Table 17
Mean, Standard Deviation and 't' values of Leadership Styles of Lower Level Executives of LIC and CBB as perceived by their themselves

Leadership Styles	*LIC Lower Level*			*CBB Lower Level*			*'t' value*
	Mean	*N*	*S.D.*	*Mean*	*N*	*S.D*	
Authoritarian (A)	21.200	40	4.937	20.916	107	4.398	0.32
Participative (P)	25.575	40	3.637	25.458	107	2.593	0.187
Bureaucratic (B)	23.250	40	3.888	23.748	107	4.402	0.666
Task-orien tation (T)	26.325	40	2.401	25.056	107	2.306	0.884
Nurturant (N)	27.375	40	2.250	26.308	107	2.860	2.371

Source: Compiled from field survey

different leadership styles of employees of LIC and CBB in self perception about their styles is rejected in Task-orientation and nurturant style and is accepted in all other cases.

For 't' value, the degree of freedom (df) is N_1+N_2-2. In LIC, Lower Level Executives stood 40 where $N_1=40$, in CBB Lower Level Executives stood 107, where $N_2=107$, the $df=N_1+N_2-2 \Rightarrow 40+107-2=145$. For 145 df the entries at 0.01 and 0.05 by linear interpolation are 2.576 and 1.960. The 't' values with two stars are significant at 0.01 level and those with one star at 0.05 level.

THE DIFFERENCE BETWEEN LEADERSHIP STYLES OF EMPLOYEES OF LIC AND CBB AS PERCEIVED BY THEIR SUBORDINATES

The difference between leadership styles of Higher Level Executives of LIC and CBB as perceived by their subordinates

Table 18 presents mean, standard deviation and 't' values of the leadership styles as perceived by their subordinates Higher Level Executives of LIC and CBB. Mean values of participative,

Table 18
Mean, Standard Deviation and 't' values of Leadership Styles of Higher Level Executives of LIC and CBB as perceived by their subordinates

Leadership Styles	*LIC Top Level*			*CBB Higher Level*			*'t' value*
	Mean	*N*	*S.D.*	*Mean*	*N*	*S.D*	
Authoritarian (A)	17.204	49	4.449	21.529	34	4.336	4.422
Participative (P)	22.204	49	3.247	22.029	34	4.489	0.194
Bureaucratic (B)	22.082	49	3.829	21.706	34	4.462	0.4
Task-orien tation (T)	23.673	49	3.112	21.941	34	4.735	1.87
Nurturant (N)	23.673	49	3.986	22.735	34	4.259	1.013

Source: Compiled from field survey

bureaucratic, task-orientation and nurturant styles are higher in Higher Level Executives of LIC than Higher Level Executives of CBB whereas mean value of authoritative style is higher in Higher Level Executives of CBB than Higher Level Executives of LIC. In participative, bureaucratic, task-orientation and nurturant styles, the Higher Level Executives of LIC and CBB do not differ significantly as the 't' values of these styles are less than the critical value (A0.199, P<0.05; P0.4, P<0.05; B1.87, P<0.05; T1.017, P<0.05 and N0.315, P<0.05). In authoritarian style, the higher level executives of LIC and CBB differ significantly as the 't' value is greater than the critical value (A4.422, P<0.01). Hence, the hypothesis, that there is no significant difference among different leadership styles of employees of LIC and CBB as perceived by their subordinates is rejected in authoritarian style an is accepted in all other cases.

For 't' value, the degree of freedom (df) is N_1+N_2-2. In LIC, Higher Level Executives subordinates stood 49 where $N_1=49$, in CBB Higher Level Executives subordinates stood 34, where $N_2=34$, the $df=N_1+N_2-2 \Rightarrow 49+34-2=81$. For 81 df the entries at 0.01 and 0.05 by linear interpolation are 2.660 and 2.000. The 't' values with two stars are significant at 0.01 level and those with one star at 0.05 level.

The difference between leadership styles of Middle Level Executives of LIC and CBB as perceived by their subordinates

Table 19 presents mean, standard deviation and 't' values of the leadership styles as perceived by their subordinates Middle Level Executives of LIC and CBB. Mean value of bureaucratic style is higher in Middle Level Executives of LIC than Middle Level Executives of CBB whereas mean value of authoritative, participative, task-orientation and nurturant styles are higher in Middle Level Executives of CBB than Middle Level

Table 19

Mean, Standard Deviation and 't' values of Leadership Styles of Middle Level Executives of LIC and CBB as perceived by their subordinates

Leadership Styles	*LIC Middle*			*CBB Middle Level*			*'t' value*
	Mean	*N*	*S.D.*	*Mean*	*N*	*S.D*	
Authoritarian (A)	16.050	40	5.063	21.841	107	5.448	6.045
Participative (P)	23.025	40	4.172	23.495	107	3.730	0.625
Bureaucratic (B)	26.000	40	2.792	23.047	107	3.820	5.127
Task-orien tation (T)	24.150	40	3.512	24.673	107	2.818	0.845
Nurturant (N)	23.325	40	4.002	26.495	107	9.165	2.911

Source: Compiled from field survey

Executives of LIC. In participative, task-orientation styles, the Middle Level Executives of LIC and CBB do not differ significantly as the 't' values of these styles are less than the critical value (P0.625, P<0.05; T0.845, P<0.05. In authoritarian, bureaucratic and nurturant styles, the middle level of LIC and CBB differ significantly as the 't' value are greater than the critical value (A6.045, P<0.01; B5.127, P<0.01; N2.911, P<0.01). Hence, the hypothesis, that there is no significant difference among different leadership styles of employees of LIC and CBB as perceived by their subordinates is accepted.

For 't' value, the degree of freedom (df) is N_1+N_2-2. In LIC, Middle Level Executives subordinates stood 40 where $N_1=40$, in CBB Middle Level Executives subordinates stood 107, where $N_2=107$, the df=N_1+N_2-2=>40+107-2=145. For 145 df the entries at 0.01 and 0.05 by linear interpolation are 2.576 and 1.960. The 't' values with two stars are significant at 0.01 level and those with one star at 0.05 level.

The difference between leadership styles of Lower Level Executives of LIC and CBB as perceived by their subordinates

Table 20 presents mean, standard deviation and 't' values of the leadership styles as perceived by their subordinates Lower Level Executives of LIC and CBB. Mean values of participative, bureaucratic and nurturant styles are higher in Lower Level Executives of LIC than Lower Level Executives of CBB whereas mean values of authoritative, task-orientation styles are higher

Table 20
Mean, Standard Deviation and 't' values of Leadership Styles of Lower Level Executives of LIC and CBB as perceived by subordinates

Leadership Styles	*LIC Junior Level*			*CBB Lower Level*			*'t' value*
	Mean	*N*	*S.D.*	*Mean*	*N*	*S.D*	
Authoritarian (A)	18.030	202	4.361	20.024	329	5.777	4.511
Participative (P)	22.520	202	3.923	22.444	329	4.590	0.203
Bureaucratic (B)	23.426	202	4.423	21.447	329	4.063	2.556
Task-orien tation (T)	23.020	202	3.007	23.033	329	4.078	0.042
Nurturant (N)	23.257	202	3.080	22.432	329	4.393	2.539

Source: Compiled from field survey

in Lower Level Executives of CBB than Lower Level Executives of LIC. In participative, task-orientation styles, the Lower Level Executives of LIC and CBB do not differ significantly as the 't' values of these styles are less than the critical value (P0.842, P<0.05; T0.972, P<0.05. In authoritarian, bureaucratic and nurturant styles, the lower level of LIC and CBB differ significantly as the 't' value are greate than the critical value. (A4.511, P<0.01; B2.556, P<0.01; N2.539, P<0.01). Hence, the hypothesis, that there is no significant difference among different leadership styles of employees of LIC and CBB as perceived by their subordinates is accepted.

For 't' value, the degree of freedom (df) is N_1+N_2-2. In LIC, Lower Level Executives subordinates stood 202 where $N_1=202$, in CBB Lower Level Executives subordinates stood 329, where $N_2=329$, the df=N_1+N_2-2=>202+329-2=529. For 529 df the entries at 0.01 and 0.05 by linear interpolation are 2.576 and 1.960. The 't' values with two stars are significant at 0.01 level and those with one star at 0.05 level.

7

THE IMPACT OF LEADERSHIP ON MOTIVATION IN INSURANCE AND BANKING SECTOR

INTRODUCTION

In order to know the difference of impact of leadership on motivation among the employees of LIC and CBB the data is interpreted and presented in the following paragraphs:

The objectives of the study is to find out the difference of impact of leadership on motivation among the employees of LIC and CBB.

The data pertain to know the following findings.

1. The difference of impact of leadership on motivation between LIC and CBB employees;
2. The difference between impact of leadership on motivation of LIC and CBB employees viz., Higher Level Executives, Middle Level Executives, Lower Level Executives and Clerks; and
3. The difference between impact of leadership on motivation of LIC and CBB at inter levels of employees viz., Higher Level Executives and Middle Level Executives, Middle Level Executives and Lower Level Executives, Lower Level Executives and Clerks.

THE IMPACT OF LEADERSHIP ON MOTIVATION OF LIC AND CBB EMPLOYEES

Impact of leadership on Motivation of LIC and CBB of Employees

Table 1, reveals that the LIC employees have shown higher impact of leadership on motivation than the CBB employees as the mean score of LIC employees (147.604) is being higher than the mean score of the CBB employees (138.092). As the calculated 't' value 4.886 is greater than the critical value, it is significant at 0.01 level. Hence, the hypothesis, that there is no significant difference between LIC and CBB employees in impact of leadership on motivation is rejected.

Table 1
Impact of Leadership on Motivation in LIC and CBB Employees

Sector	*N*	*Mean*	*S.D.*	*'t' value*
LIC	300	147.604	25.747	4.866
CBB	500	138.092	28.379	

Source: Compiled from field survey

For 't' value, the degree of freedom (df) is N_1+N_2-2. In LIC, employees stood 300 where $N_1=300$, in CBB, employees stood 500, where $N_2=500$, the $df=N_1+N_2-2 => 300+500-2=798$. For 798 df the entries at 0.01 and 0.05 by linear interpolation are 2.576 and 1.960. The 't' values with two stars are significant at 0.01 level and those with one star at 0.05 level.

Impact of Leadership on Motivation of Higher Level Executives of LIC and CBB

Table 2, reveals that the LIC Higher Level Executives have shown higher impact of leadership on motivation than the CBB Higher Level Executives as the mean score of LIC Higher Level Executives (151.111) is being higher than the mean score of the CBB Higher Level Executives (138.667). As the calculated 't' value 1.891 is less than the critical value, it is not significant at 0.05 level. Hence, the hypothesis, that there is no significant difference between LIC and CBB employees in impact of leadership on motivation is accepted.

Table 2
Impact of Leadership on Motivation in LIC and CBB Higher Level Executives

Sector	*N*	*Mean*	*S.D.*	*'t' value*
LIC	9	151.111	15.479	1.891
CBB	30	138.667	22.387	

Source: Compiled from field survey

For 't' value, the degree of freedom (df) is N_1+N_2-2. In LIC, Higher Level Executives stood 9 where $N_1=9$, in CBB, Higher Level Executives stood 30, where $N_2=30$, the df=N_1+N_2-2=>9+30-2=37. For 37 df the entries at 0.01 and 0.05 by linear interpolation are 2.042 and 2.750. The 't' values with two stars are significant at 0.01 level and those with one star at 0.05 level.

Impact of Leadership on Motivation of Middle Level Executives of LIC and CBB

Table 3, reveals that the LIC Middle Level Executives have shown higher impact of leadership on motivation than the CBB Middle Level Executives as the mean score of LIC Middle Level Executives (146.184) is being higher than the mean score of the CBB Middle Level Executives (134.500). As the calculated 't' value 1.979 is less than the critical value, it is not significant at 0.05 level. Hence, the hypothesis, that there is no significant difference between LIC and CBB employees in impact of leadership on motivation is accepted.

Table 3
Impact of Leadership on Motivation in LIC and CBB Middle Level Executives

Sector	*N*	*Mean*	*S.D.*	*'t' value*
LIC	49	146.184	23.797	1.979
CBB	34	134.500	28.137	

Source: Compiled from field survey

For 't' value, the degree of freedom (df) is N_1+N_2-2. In LIC, Middle Level Executives stood 49 where $N_1=49$, in CBB,

THE IMPACT OF LEADERSHIP ON MOTIVATION OF LIC AND CBB EMPLOYEES

Impact of leadership on Motivation of LIC and CBB of Employees

Table 1, reveals that the LIC employees have shown higher impact of leadership on motivation than the CBB employees as the mean score of LIC employees (147.604) is being higher than the mean score of the CBB employees (138.092). As the calculated 't' value 4.886 is greater than the critical value, it is significant at 0.01 level. Hence, the hypothesis, that there is no significant difference between LIC and CBB employees in impact of leadership on motivation is rejected.

Table 1
Impact of Leadership on Motivation in LIC and CBB Employees

Sector	*N*	*Mean*	*S.D.*	*'t' value*
LIC	300	147.604	25.747	4.866
CBB	500	138.092	28.379	

Source: Compiled from field survey

For 't' value, the degree of freedom (df) is N_1+N_2-2. In LIC, employees stood 300 where $N_1=300$, in CBB, employees stood 500, where $N_2=500$, the df=N_1+N_2-2=>300+500-2=798. For 798 df the entries at 0.01 and 0.05 by linear interpolation are 2.576 and 1.960. The 't' values with two stars are significant at 0.01 level and those with one star at 0.05 level.

Impact of Leadership on Motivation of Higher Level Executives of LIC and CBB

Table 2, reveals that the LIC Higher Level Executives have shown higher impact of leadership on motivation than the CBB Higher Level Executives as the mean score of LIC Higher Level Executives (151.111) is being higher than the mean score of the CBB Higher Level Executives (138.667). As the calculated 't' value 1.891 is less than the critical value, it is not significant at 0.05 level. Hence, the hypothesis, that there is no significant difference between LIC and CBB employees in impact of leadership on motivation is accepted.

Table 2
Impact of Leadership on Motivation in LIC and CBB Higher Level Executives

Sector	*N*	*Mean*	*S.D.*	*'t' value*
LIC	9	151.111	15.479	1.891
CBB	30	138.667	22.387	

Source: Compiled from field survey

For 't' value, the degree of freedom (df) is N_1+N_2-2. In LIC, Higher Level Executives stood 9 where $N_1=9$, in CBB, Higher Level Executives stood 30, where $N_2=30$, the df=N_1+N_2-2=>9+30-2=37. For 37 df the entries at 0.01 and 0.05 by linear interpolation are 2.042 and 2.750. The 't' values with two stars are significant at 0.01 level and those with one star at 0.05 level.

Impact of Leadership on Motivation of Middle Level Executives of LIC and CBB

Table 3, reveals that the LIC Middle Level Executives have shown higher impact of leadership on motivation than the CBB Middle Level Executives as the mean score of LIC Middle Level Executives (146.184) is being higher than the mean score of the CBB Middle Level Executives (134.500). As the calculated 't' value 1.979 is less than the critical value, it is not significant at 0.05 level. Hence, the hypothesis, that there is no significant difference between LIC and CBB employees in impact of leadership on motivation is accepted.

Table 3
Impact of Leadership on Motivation in LIC and CBB Middle Level Executives

Sector	*N*	*Mean*	*S.D.*	*'t' value*
LIC	49	146.184	23.797	1.979
CBB	34	134.500	28.137	

Source: Compiled from field survey

For 't' value, the degree of freedom (df) is N_1+N_2-2. In LIC, Middle Level Executives stood 49 where $N_1=49$, in CBB,

Middle Level Executives stood 34, where N_2=34, the df=N_1+N_2-2=>49+34-2=81. For 81 df the entries at 0.01 and 0.05 by linear interpolation are 2.660 and 2.000. The 't' values with two stars are significant at 0.01 level and those with one star at 0.05 level.

Impact of Leadership on Motivation of Lower Level Executives of LIC and CBB

Table 4, reveals that the LIC Lower Level Executives have shown higher impact of leadership on motivation than the CBB Lower Level Executives as the mean score of LIC Lower Level Executives (158.525) is being higher than the mean score of the CBB Lower Level Executives (150.449). As the calculated 't' value 1.713 is less than the critical value, it is not significant at 0.05 level. Hence, the hypothesis, that there is no significant difference between LIC and CBB employees in impact of leadership on motivation is accepted.

Table 4
Impact of Leadership on Motivation in LIC and CBB Lower Level Executives

Sector	*N*	*Mean*	*S.D.*	*'t' value*
LIC	40	158.525	23.669	1.713
CBB	107	150.449	29.686	

Source: Compiled from field survey

For 't' value, the degree of freedom (df) is N_1+N_2-2. In LIC, Lower Level Executives stood 40 where N_1=40, in CBB, Lower Level Executives stood 107, where N_2=107, the df=N_1+N_2-2=>40+107-2=145. For 145 df the entries at 0.01 and 0.05 by linear interpolation are 2.576 and 1.960. The 't' values with two stars are significant at 0.01 level and those with one star at 0.05 level.

Impact of Leadership on Motivation of Clerks of LIC and CBB

Table 5, reveals that the LIC Clerks have shown higher impact of leadership on motivation than the CBB Clerks as the mean score of LIC Clerks (145.604) is being higher than the mean score of the CBB Clerks (134.392). As the calculated 't' value

4.668 is greater than the critical value, it is significant at 0.01 level. Hence, the hypothesis, that there is no significant difference between LIC and CBB employees in impact of leadership on motivation is rejected.

Table 5
Impact of Leadership on Motivation in LIC and CBB Clerks

Sector	N	Mean	S.D.	't' value
LIC	202	145.604	26.531	4.668
CBB	329	134.392	27.414	

Source: Compiled from field survey

For 't' value, the degree of freedom (df) is N_1+N_2-2. In LIC, Clerks stood 202 where $N_1=202$, in CBB, Clerks stood 329, where $N_2=329$, the df=N_1+N_2-2=>202+329-2=529. For 529 df the entries at 0.01 and 0.05 by linear interpolation are 2.576 and 1.960. The 't' values with two stars are significant at 0.01 level and those with one star at 0.05 level.

Impact of Leadership on Motivation of Higher Level Executives and Middle Level Executives of LIC

Table 6, reveals that the LIC Higher Level Executives have shown higher impact of leadership on motivation than the LIC Middle Level Executives as the mean score of LIC Higher Level Executives (151.111) is being higher than the mean score of the LIC Middle Level Executives (146.184). As the calculated 't' value 0.797 is less than the critical value, it is not significant at 0.05 level. Hence, the hypothesis, that there is no significant difference between employees of LIC in impact of leadership on motivation is accepted.

Table 6
Impact of Leadership on Motivation in LIC Higher Level Executives and Middle Level Executives

Job Level	*N*	*Mean*	*S.D.*	*'t' value*
Higher Level Executives	9	151.111	15.479	0.797
Middle Level Executives	49	146.184	23.797	

Source: Compiled from field survey

For 't' value, the degree of freedom (df) is N_1+N_2-2. In LIC, Higher Level Executives stood 9 where $N_1=9$, Middle Level Executives stood 49, where $N_2=49$, the df=N_1+N_2-2=>9+49-2=56. For 56 df the entries at 0.01 and 0.05 by linear interpolation are 2.704 and 2.021. The 't' values with two stars are significant at 0.01 level and those with one star at 0.05 level.

Impact of Leadership on Motivation of Middle Level Executives and Lower Level Executives of LIC

Table 7, reveals that the LIC Lower Level Executives have shown higher impact of leadership on motivation than the LIC Middle Level Executives as the mean score of LIC Lower Level Executives (158.525) is being higher than the mean score of the LIC Middle Level Executives (146.184). As the calculated 't' value 2.441 is greater than the critical value, it is significant at 0.05 level. Hence, the hypothesis, that there is no significant difference between employees of LIC in impact of leadership on motivation is rejected.

Table 7
Impact of Leadership on Motivation in LIC Middle Level Executives and Lower Level Executives

Job Level	*N*	*Mean*	*S.D.*	*'t' value*
Middle Level Executives	49	146.184	23.797	2.441
Lower Level Executives	40	158.525	23.669	

Source: Compiled from field survey

For 't' value, the degree of freedom (df) is N_1+N_2-2. In LIC, Middle Level Executives stood 49 where $N_1=49$, Lower Level Executives stood 40, where $N_2=40$, the df=N_1+N_2-2=>49+40-2=87. For 87 df the entries at 0.01 and 0.05 by linear interpolation are 2.660 and 2.000. The 't' values with two stars are significant at 0.01 level and those with one star at 0.05 level.

Impact of Leadership on Motivation of Lower Level Executives and Clerks of LIC

Table 8, reveals that the LIC Lower Level Executives have shown higher impact of leadership on motivation than the LIC

Clerks as the mean score of LIC Lower Level Executives (158.525) is being higher than the mean score of the LIC Clerks (145.604). As the calculated 't' value 3.09 is greater than the critical value, it is significant at 0.01 level. Hence, the hypothesis, that that there is no significant difference between employees of LIC in impact of leadership on motivation is rejected.

Table 8
Impact of Leadership on Motivation in LIC Lower Level Executives and Clerks

Job Level	*N*	*Mean*	*S.D.*	*'t' value*
Lower Level Executives	40	158.525	23.669	0.003
Clerks	202	145.604	26.531	

Source: Compiled from field survey

For 't' value, the degree of freedom (df) is N_1+N_2-2. In LIC, Lower Level Executives stood 40 where $N_1=40$, Clerks stood 202, where $N_2=202$, the df=N_1+N_2-2=>40+202-2=240. For 240 df the entries at 0.01 and 0.05 by linear interpolation are 2.576 and 1.960. The 't' values with two stars are significant at 0.01 level and those with one star at 0.05 level.

Impact of Leadership on Motivation of Higher Level Executives and Middle Level Executives of CBB

Table 9, reveals that the CBB Higher Level Executives have shown higher impact of leadership on motivation than the CBB Middle Level Executives as the mean score of CBB Higher Level Executives (138.667) is being higher than the mean score of the CBB Middle Level Executives (134.500). As the calculated

Table 9
Impact of Leadership on Motivation in CBB Higher Level Executives and Middle Level Executives

Job Level	*N*	*Mean*	*S.D.*	*'t' value*
Higher Level Executives	30	138.667	22.387	0.659
Middle Level Executives	34	134.500	28.137	

Source: Compiled from field survey

't' value 0.659 is less than the critical value, it is not significant at 0.05 level. Hence, the hypothesis, that there is no significant difference between employees of CBB in impact of leadership on motivation is accepted.

For 't' value, the degree of freedom (df) is N_1+N_2-2. In CBB, Higher Level Executives stood 30 where $N_1=30$, Middle Level Executives stood 34, where $N_2=34$, the df=N_1+N_2-2=>30+34-2=62. For 62 df the entries at 0.01 and 0.05 by linear interpolation are 2.704 and 2.021. The 't' values with two stars are significant at 0.01 level and those with one star at 0.05 level.

Impact of Leadership on Motivation of Middle Level Executives and Lower Level Executives of CBB

Table 10, reveals that the CBB Lower Level Executives have shown higher impact of leadership on motivation than the CBB Middle Level Executives as the mean score of CBB Lower Level Executives (150.449) is being higher than the mean score of the CBB Middle Level Executives (134.500). As the calculated 't' value 2.841 is greater than the critical value, it is significant at 0.01 level. Hence, the hypothesis, that there is no significant difference between employees of CBB in impact of leadership on motivation is rejected.

Table 10
Impact of Leadership on Motivation in CBB Middle Level Executives and Lower Level Executives

Job Level	*N*	*Mean*	*S.D.*	*'t' value*
Middle Level Executives	34	134.500	28.137	2.841
Lower Level Executives	107	150.449	29.686	

Source: Compiled from field survey

For 't' value, the degree of freedom (df) is N_1+N_2-2. In CBB, Middle Level Executives stood 34 where $N_1=34$, Lower Level Executives stood 107, where $N_2=107$, the df=N_1+N_2-2=>34 +107-2=139. For 139 df the entries at 0.01 and 0.05 by linear interpolation are 2.576 and 1.960. The 't' values with two stars are significant at 0.01 level and those with one star at 0.05 level.

Impact of Leadership on Motivation of Lower Level Executives and Clerks of CBB

Table 11, reveals that the CBB Lower Level Executives have shown higher impact of leadership on motivation than the Clerks as the mean score of CBB Lower Level Executives (150.449) is being higher than the mean score of the Clerks (134.392). As the calculated 't' value 4.95 is greater than the critical value, it is significant at 0.01 level. Hence, the hypothesis, that there is no significant difference between employees of CBB in impact of leadership on motivation is rejected.

Table 11
Impact of Leadership on Motivation in CBB Lower Level Executives and Clerks

Job Level	*N*	*Mean*	*S.D.*	*'t' value*
Lower Level Executives	107	150.449	29.686	4.95
Clerks	329	134.392	27.414	

Source: Compiled from field survey

For 't' value, the degree of freedom (df) is N_1+N_2-2. In CBB, Lower Level Executives stood 107where $N_1=107$, Clerks stood 329, where $N_2=329$, the df=N_1+N_2-2=>107+329-2=434. For 434 df the entries at 0.01 and 0.05 by linear interpolation are 2.576 and 1.960. The 't' values with two stars are significant at 0.01 level and those with one star at 0.05 level.

DEGREE OF IMPACT OF LEADERSHIP ON MOTIVATION OF LIC AND CBB EMPLOYEES

The degree of impact of leadership on motivation of employees is classified as high, moderate and low. The scores of the employees are arranged in descending order. The top 27 per cent of the sample employees is categorized as high and the bottom 27 per cent as low. The remaining employees come under the moderate category.

Impact of Leadership on Motivation of LIC and CBB Employees Under their High Degree of Motivation

Table 12, reveals that the LIC employees under High Degree of Impact of leadership on Motivation have shown higher Impact of leadership on motivation than the CBB employees under High Degree of Impact of Motivation as the mean score of LIC employees (178.086) is being higher than the mean score of the CBB employees (168.037). As the calculated 't' value 3.059 is greater than the critical value, it is significant at 0.01 level. Hence, the hypothesis, that there is no significant difference between LIC and CBB employees under their high degree of Impact of leadership on motivation is rejected.

Table 12
High Degree of Impact of Leadership on Motivation of LIC and CBB Employees

Sector	*N*	*Mean*	*S.D.*	*t' value*
LIC	81	178.086	11.1	3.050
CBB	135	168.037	15.43	

Source: Compiled from field survey

For 't' value, the degree of freedom (df) is N_1+N_2-2. In LIC, High Degree of Impact of Motivation of LIC employees stood 81 where $N_1=81$, High Degree of Impact of Motivation of CBB employees stood 135, where $N_2=135$, the df=N_1+N_2-2=>81+135-2=214. For 214 df the entries at 0.01 and 0.05 by linear interpolation are 2.576 and 1.960. The 't' values with two stars are significant at 0.01 level and those with one star at 0.05 level.

Impact of Leadership on Motivation of LIC and CBB Employees Under their Low Degree of Motivation

Table 13, reveals that the LIC employees under Low Degree of Impact of Motivation have shown higher Impact of leadership on motivation than the CBB employees under Low Degree of Impact of leadership on Motivation as the mean score of LIC employees (115.84) is being higher than the mean score of the CBB employees (101.237). As the calculated 't' value

5.97 is greater than the critical value, it is significant at 0.01 level. Hence, the hypothesis, that there is no significant difference between LIC and CBB employees under their low degree of Impact of leadership on motivation is rejected.

Table 13
Low Degree of Impact of Leadership on Motivation of LIC and CBB Employees

Sector	*N*	*Mean*	*S.D.*	*t' value*
LIC	81	115.84	17.02	5.97
CBB	135	101.237	18.02	

Source: Compiled from field survey

For 't' value, the degree of freedom (df) is N_1+N_2-2. In LIC, Low Degree of Impact of Motivation of LIC employees stood 81 where N=81, Low Degree of Impact of Motivation of CBB employees stood 135, where $N_2=135$, the df=N_1+N_2-2=>81+135-2=214. For 214 df the entries at 0.01 and 0.05 by linear interpolation are 2.576 and 1.960. The 't' values with two stars are significant at 0.01 level and those with one star at 0.05 level.

Impact of Leadership on Motivation of LIC and CBB Employees Under their Moderate Degree of Motivation

Table 14, reveals that the LIC employees under Moderate Degree of Impact of leadership on Motivation have shown higher Impact of motivation than the CBB employees under Moderate Degree of Impact of leadership on Motivation as the mean score of LIC employees (148.319) is being higher than the mean score of the CBB employees (142.148). As the calculated 't' value 7.005 is greater than the critical value, it is significant at 0.01 level. Hence, the hypothesis, that there is no significant difference between LIC and CBB employees under their Moderate degree of Impact of leadership on motivation is rejected.

For 't' value, the degree of freedom (df) is N_1+N_2-2. In LIC, Moderate Degree of Impact of Motivation of LIC employees stood 138 where $N_1=138$, Moderate Degree of

Table 14
Moderate Degree of Impact of Leadership on Motivation of LIC and CBB Employees

Sector	*N*	*Mean*	*S.D.*	*t' value*
LIC	138	148.319	7.704	7.005
CBB	230	142.148	8.922	

Source: Compiled from field survey

Impact of Motivation of CBB employees stood 230, where N_2=230, the df=N_1+N_2-2=>138+230-2=366. For 366 df the entries at 0.01 and 0.05 by linear interpolation are 2.576 and 1.960. The 't' values with two stars are significant at 0.01 level and those with one star at 0.05 level.

8

SUMMARY OF FINDINGS AND CONCLUSIONS

INTRODUCTION

The importance of motivation and leadership in organisational setting have been well recognized and a serious thought is extended by theoreticians and practitioners from all disciplines. As a result many researchers have been conducted and varied conclusions have been drawn on the basis of their findings. A common denominator in all the findings of differenr studies has been that, higher the level of motivation greater the efficiency and effectiveness in organisational performance. Nevertheless, the process of motivation is closely related to the process and the practices of leadership in organisations. Thus, the study of motivation will be incomplete without leadership and vise versa. The present study is also designed in the same pattern covering the employees of LIC and CBB in Nellore District.

The summary of the findings of the III to VII chapters of the study is presented in the following paragraphs. The main objectives of the present study is to investigate whether there is a relationship between SEOP variables and motivation, between SEOP variables and leadership styles, between self and subordinates perception of leadership styles, between SEOP variables and impact of the leadership on motivation of employees in LIC and CBB.

SUMMARY

Motivation and Leadership are closely related to various other aspects like job satisfaction and communication. Motivation and Leadership are a process of influencing the behaviour, beliefs and feelings of the members of a group. The function of leadership however, cover a wide range of activities like coordinating, decision making, policy making, group representing, controlling, arbitrating etc. Leadership is affected by many variables and involves with several skills like conceptual, designing, technical, human, creative and communicative. The effectiveness of leadership adumbrates the personality of the leader, past experience; expectations of superiors; the characteristics of subordinates; the requirements of the tasks; and the organisational climate and policies.

Motivation is the resultant feeling of the employee. It is the function of the expectation of individual and potentiality of the job to achieve the fulfillment of the needs. Motivation, thus, refers to the individual's complex reaction towards his job which is primarily based upon the satisfaction of the objectivity of needs. Measurement of motivation, is affected by a wide range of variables relating to individual, social, cultural, organisational and environmental factors. The concept of motivation has been related with other concepts like absenteeism, labour turnover, meaningful work, technology, psychological well being and productivity.

In the 21st century, several theories have been profounded to understand its significance, process and impact on employees of organisations. The theories such as Maslow's need hierarchy theory, Herzberg's two factor theory and Vroom's valance instrumentality expectancy theory were developed to explain work motivation.

The Leadership is equally a complex concept having a bearing on motivation, morale, organisational climate, human relations and communication. Beginning with scientific management the organisational leadership has been emphasized in human resource approach too. Leadership theories can be classified as trait theory, bahavioural theory and contingency theory. The trait theory has been put to rigorous research by Byrd, Gennings, Stogdill etc., and resulted in the development of behavioural theory. The Ohio state study, Michigon study, Managerial grid, Likerts theory, Mc Gregor X and Y theory have opened new vistas on the behavioural dimensions of leadership. The controversy of trait and behavioural theories have given lead to the contingency models of leadership like Fiedler's contingency model, Vroom and Yetton contingency model, Path goal theory, Life cycle theory, Tri-dimensional model, Learning model etc.

FINDINGS

I. The following are major findings of this study on motivation.

1. There is significant difference between the motivation of the employees of Life Insurance Corporation of India and Commercial Bank Branches.
2. There is significant difference between the motivation of the Higher Level Executives of LIC and CBB.
3. There is significant difference between the motivation of the Middle Level Executives of LIC and CBB.
4. There is significant difference between the motivation of the Lower Level Executives of LIC and CBB.
5. There is significant difference between the motivation of Clerical employees of LIC and CBB.
6. There is significant difference between Higher Level and Middle Level Executives of LIC in motivation.
7. There is significant difference between Middle Level and Lower Level Executives of LIC in motivation.
8. There is significant difference between Lower Level Executives and Clerical Employees of LIC in motivation.
9. There is significant difference between Higher Level Executives and Middle Level Executives of CBB in motivation.
10. There is significant difference between Middle Level Executives and Lower Level Executives of CBB in motivation.

11. There is significant difference between Lower Level Executives and Clerical Employees of CBB in motivation.
12. There is significant difference between LIC and CBB Employees under their high degree of motivation.
13. There is significant difference between LIC and CBB Employees under their low degree of motivation
14. There is significant difference between LIC and CBB Employees under their moderate degree of motivation.

II. The following are major findings of leader's self perception.

1. In LIC, among Higher Level Executives, a significant inter relationship among socio–economic and organization position variables (SEOP) is found in the case of age Vs education and experience Vs education and no significant inter relationship is found among other SEOP variables.

   In CBB, among Higher Level Executives, a significant inter relationship among SEOP variables is found in the case of designation Vs experience, age Vs experience and age Vs education and no significant inter relationship is found among other SEOP variables.

2. In LIC, among Middle Level Executives, a significant inter relationship among SEOP variables is found in the case of age vs experience, age vs education, age vs economic status and experience vs education and no significant inter relationship is found among other SEOP variables.

   In CBB, among Middle Level Executives, a significant inter relationship among SEOP variables is found in the case of age vs experience and no significant inter relationship is found among other SEOP variables.

3. In LIC, among Lower Level Executives, a significant inter relationship among SEOP variables is found in the case of designation Vs economic status, age Vs experience, age Vs education and experience Vs economic status and no significant inter relationship is found among other SEOP variables.

In CBB, among Lower Level Executives, a significant inter relationship among SEOP variables is found in the case of age vs experience and no significant inter relationship is found among other SEOP variables.

4. In LIC, among Clerical Level, a significant inter relationship among SEOP variables is found in the case of age vs experience and experience vs education and no significant inter relationship is found among other SEOP variables.

   In CBB, among Clerical Level, a significant inter relationship among SEOP variables is found in the case of age vs experience, age vs education, experience vs education and education vs economic status and no significant inter relationship is found among other SEOP variables.

5. In LIC, among the Higher Level Executives, a significant relationship between SEOP variables and leadership styles is found in the case of 'age' vs 'nurturant', 'experience' vs 'bureaucratic', 'experience' vs 'task-orientation', 'experience' vs 'nurturant', 'education' vs 'bureaucratic'and 'education' vs 'nurturant' 'economic status' vs 'authoritarian' and no significant relationship is found between other SEOP variables and leadership styles.

   In CBB, among the Higher Level Executives, a significant relationship between SEOP variables and leadership styles is found in the case of 'age' vs 'authoritarian', 'age' vs 'task-orientation', 'experience' vs 'participative', 'experience' vs 'nurturant', 'education' vs 'authoritarian', 'education' vs 'task-orientation' 'education' vs 'nurturant', and 'economic status' vs 'authoritarian' 'economic status' vs 'participative' and no significant relationship is found between other SEOP variables and leadership styles .

6. In LIC, among the Middle Level Executives, a significant relationship between SEOP variables and leadership styles is found in the case of 'age' vs 'bureaucratic', and 'education' vs 'nurturant' and no significant relationship is found between other SEOP variables and leadership styles .

In CBB, among the Middle Level Executives, a significant relationship between SEOP variables and leadership styles does not exist.

7. In LIC, among the Lower Level Executives, a significant relationship between SEOP variables and leadership styles is found in the case of 'experience' vs 'task-orientation', 'education' vs 'participative', 'education' vs 'bureaucratic' 'economic status' vs 'task-orientation' 'economic status' vs 'nurturant' and no significant relationship is found between other SEOP variables and leadership styles .

   In CBB, among the Lower Level Executives, a significant relationship between SEOP variables and leadership styles is found in the case of 'economic status' vs 'participative' and no significant relationship is found between other SEOP variables and leadership styles .

8. In LIC, at Higher Level Executives, a significant inter relationship among leadership styles is found in the case of 'participative' vs 'task-orientation', 'bureaucratic' vs 'nurturant' and 'task-orientation' vs 'nurturant' and no significant inter relationship is found among other leadership styles.

   In CBB, at Higher Level Executives, a significant inter relationship among leadership styles is found in the case of 'authoritarian' vs 'participative', 'authoritarian' vs 'task-orientation', 'authoritarian' vs 'nurturant', 'participative' vs 'task-orientation', 'participative' vs 'nurturant', 'bureaucratic' vs 'task orientation', and 'task-orientation' vs 'nurturant' and no significant inter relationship is found among other leadership styles .

9. In LIC, at Middle Level Executives, a significant inter relationship among leadership styles is found in the case of 'authoritarian' vs 'bureaucratic', 'authoritarian' vs 'nurturant', 'participative' vs 'nurturant', 'bureaucratic' vs 'task-orientation' and 'task-orientation' vs 'nurturant' and no significant inter relationship is found among other leadership styles .

In CBB, at Middle Level Executives, a significant inter relationship among leadership styles is found in the case of 'authoritarian' vs 'bureaucratic', 'authoritarian' vs 'nurturant', 'participative' vs 'task-orientation', 'participative' vs 'nurturant', 'bureaucratic' vs 'task-orientation', 'bureaucratic' vs 'nurturant', and 'task-orientation' vs 'nurturant' and no significant inter relationship is found among other leadership styles .

10. In LIC, at Lower Level Executives, a significant inter relationship among leadership styles is found in the case of 'authoritarian' vs 'bureaucratic', 'authoritarian' vs 'task-orientation', 'authoritarian' vs 'nurturant', 'participative' vs 'task-orientation', 'participative' vs 'nurturant', 'bureaucratic' vs 'task-orientation', 'bureaucratic' vs 'nurturant', and 'task-orientation' vs 'nurturant' and no significant inter relationship is found among other leadership styles .

In CBB, at Lower Level Executives, a significant inter relationship among leadership styles is found in the case of 'authoritarian' vs 'bureaucratic', 'participative' vs 'bureaucratic' 'participative' vs 'task-orientation', 'participative' vs 'nurturant', 'bureaucratic' vs 'task-orientation', and 'task-orientation' vs 'nurturant' and no significant inter relationship is found among other leadership styles .

III. The following are the major findings of subordinates perception on superiors leadership styles.

1. In LIC, among the Middle Level Executives, a significant relationship between SEOP variables and leadership styles is found in the case of 'experience' vs 'participative' style, 'experience' vs 'bureaucratic' style, and 'experience' vs 'nurturant' style, 'economic status' vs 'participative' style and no significant relationship is found between other SEOP variables and leadership styles.

In CBB, among the Middle Level Executives, a significant relationship between SEOP variables and leadership styles is found in the case of 'experience' vs 'participative' and

In CBB, among the Middle Level Executives, a significant relationship between SEOP variables and leadership styles does not exist.

7. In LIC, among the Lower Level Executives, a significant relationship between SEOP variables and leadership styles is found in the case of 'experience' vs 'task-orientation', 'education' vs 'participative', 'education' vs 'bureaucratic' 'economic status' vs 'task-orientation' 'economic status' vs 'nurturant' and no significant relationship is found between other SEOP variables and leadership styles .

   In CBB, among the Lower Level Executives, a significant relationship between SEOP variables and leadership styles is found in the case of 'economic status' vs 'participative' and no significant relationship is found between other SEOP variables and leadership styles .

8. In LIC, at Higher Level Executives, a significant inter relationship among leadership styles is found in the case of 'participative' vs 'task-orientation', 'bureaucratic' vs 'nurturant' and 'task-orientation' vs 'nurturant' and no significant inter relationship is found among other leadership styles.

   In CBB, at Higher Level Executives, a significant inter relationship among leadership styles is found in the case of 'authoritarian' vs 'participative', 'authoritarian' vs 'task-orientation', 'authoritarian' vs 'nurturant', 'participative' vs 'task-orientation', 'participative vs 'nurturant', 'bureaucratic' vs 'task orientation', and 'task-orientation' vs 'nurturant' and no significant inter relationship is found among other leadership styles .

9. In LIC, at Middle Level Executives, a significant inter relationship among leadership styles is found in the case of 'authoritarian' vs 'bureaucratic', 'authoritarian' vs 'nurturant', 'participative' vs 'nurturant', 'bureaucratic' vs 'task-orientation' and 'task-orientation' vs 'nurturant' and no significant inter relationship is found among other leadership styles .

In CBB, at Middle Level Executives, a significant inter relationship among leadership styles is found in the case of 'authoritarian' vs 'bureaucratic', 'authoritarian' vs 'nurturant', 'participative' vs 'task-orientation', 'participative' vs 'nurturant', 'bureaucratic' vs 'task-orientation', 'bureaucratic' vs 'nurturant', and 'task-orientation' vs 'nurturant' and no significant inter relationship is found among other leadership styles .

10. In LIC, at Lower Level Executives, a significant inter relationship among leadership styles is found in the case of 'authoritarian' vs 'bureaucratic', 'authoritarian' vs 'task-orientation', 'authoritarian' vs 'nurturant', 'participative' vs 'task-orientation', 'participative' vs 'nurturant', 'bureaucratic' vs 'task-orientation', 'bureaucratic' vs 'nurturant', and 'task-orientation' vs 'nurturant' and no significant inter relationship is found among other leadership styles .

    In CBB, at Lower Level Executives, a significant inter relationship among leadership styles is found in the case of 'authoritarian' vs 'bureaucratic', 'participative' vs 'bureaucratic' 'participative' vs 'task-orientation', 'participative' vs 'nurturant', 'bureaucratic' vs 'task-orientation', and 'task-orientation' vs 'nurturant' and no significant inter relationship is found among other leadership styles .

III. The following are the major findings of subordinates perception on superiors leadership styles.

1. In LIC, among the Middle Level Executives, a significant relationship between SEOP variables and leadership styles is found in the case of 'experience' vs 'participative' style, 'experience' vs 'bureaucratic' style, and 'experience' vs 'nurturant' style, 'economic status' vs 'participative' style and no significant relationship is found between other SEOP variables and leadership styles.

   In CBB, among the Middle Level Executives, a significant relationship between SEOP variables and leadership styles is found in the case of 'experience' vs 'participative' and no significant relationship is found between other SEOP variables and leadership styles .

2. In LIC, among the Lower Level Executives, a significant relationship between SEOP variables and leadership styles is found in the case of 'designation' vs 'authoritarian', 'age' vs 'participative', 'age' vs 'task-orientation', 'age' vs 'nurturant', 'experience' vs 'participative', 'experience' vs 'bureaucratic' style, and 'education' vs 'bureaucratic' style and no significant relationship is found between other SEOP variables and leadership styles.

   In CBB, among the Lower Level Executives, a significant relationship between SEOP variables and leadership styles is found in the case of education' vs 'bureaucratic', 'education' vs 'task-orientation', 'economic status' vs 'participative' style and no significant relationship is found between other SEOP variables and leadership styles.

3. In LIC, at Clerical Level, a significant relationship between SEOP variables and leadership styles is found in the case of 'designation' vs 'authoritarian', and 'experience' vs 'bureaucratic' style and no significant relationship is found between other SEOP variables and leadership styles .

   In CBB, at Clerical Level, a significant relationship between SEOP variables and leadership styles is found in the case of 'age' vs 'task-orientation', 'experience' vs 'task-orientation', 'education' vs 'authoritarian' 'education' vs 'participative' and 'education' vs 'nurturant' style and no significant relationship is found between other SEOP variables and leadership styles .

4. In LIC, at Middle Level Executives, a significant inter relationship among leadership styles is found in the case of 'authoritarian' vs 'participative', 'participative vs 'bureaucratic', 'participative' vs 'task-orientation', 'participative' vs 'nurturant', 'bureaucratic' vs 'task-orientation', 'bureaucratic' vs 'nurturant', and 'task-orientation' vs 'nurturant' style and no significant inter relationship is found among other leadership styles.

In CBB, at Middle Level Executives, a significant inter relationship among leadership styles is found in the case of authoritarian' vs 'task-orientation', 'participative' vs 'bureaucratic', 'participative' vs 'task-orientation', 'participative' vs 'nurturant', 'bureaucratic' vs 'task-orientation', 'bureaucratic' vs 'nurturant' and 'task-orientation' vs 'nurturant' style and no significant inter relationship is found among other leadership styles .

5. In LIC, at Lower Level Executives, a significant inter relationship among leadership styles is found in the case of 'authoritarian' vs 'task-orientation', 'authoritarian' vs 'nurturant', 'participative' vs 'task-orientation', 'participative' vs 'nurturant', and 'task-orientation' vs 'nurturant' style and no significant inter relationship is found among other leadership styles .

   In CBB, at Lower Level Executives, a significant inter relationship among leadership styles is found in the case of 'participative' vs 'bureaucratic', 'participative' vs 'task-orientation', 'participative' vs 'nurturant', 'bureaucratic' vs 'task-orientation', 'bureaucratic' vs 'nurturant' and 'task-orientation' vs 'nurturant' style and no significant inter relationship is found among other leadership styles

6. In LIC, at Clerical Level, a significant inter relationship among leadership styles is found in the case of 'authoritarian' vs 'participative', 'authoritarian' vs 'nurturant', 'participative vs 'bureaucratic', 'participative' vs 'task-orientation', 'participative' vs 'nurturant', 'bureaucratic' vs 'task-orientation', 'bureaucratic' vs 'nurturant', and 'task-orientation' vs 'nurturant' style and no significant inter relationship is found among other leadership styles

   In CBB, at Clerical Level, a significant inter relationship among leadership styles was found in all the cases.

IV. The following are the major findings of the difference leadership styles, self and subordinates perception.

(a) *The following are the major findings of the difference of leadership styles at the inter levels about their self perception.*

1. In LIC, no significant difference is found among different leadership styles at Higher Level Executives as well as Middle Level Executives and difference found in bureaucratic style.
2. In LIC, no significant difference is found among different leadership styles at Middle Level Executives as well as Lower Level Executives and difference found in bureaucratic style.
3. In CBB, no significant difference is found among different leadership styles at Higher Level Executives as well as Middle Level Executives and difference found in nurturant style.
4. In CBB, no significant difference is found among different leadership styles at Middle Level Executives as well as Lower Level Executives and difference found in authoritarian, participating and bureaucratic style.

(b) The following are the major findings of the difference of the leadership styles at inter levels as perceived by their subordinates.

5. In LIC, no significant difference is found among different leadership styles at Higher Level Executives as well as Middle Level Executives and no difference in participative style.
6. In LIC, no significant difference is found among different leadership styles at Middle Level Executives as well as Lower Level Executives and no difference in participative style.
7. In CBB, no significant difference is found among different leadership styles at Higher Level Executives as well as MIddle Level Executives and no difference in bureaucratic style.
8. In CBB, no significant difference is found among different leadership styles at Middle Level Executives as well as Lower Level Executives and difference is in task-orientation style.

(c) *The following of the major findings of the difference between leadership styles as judged by leader himself and as judged by his immediate subordinate's at different levels.*

9. In LIC, no significant difference is found in leadership styles at Higher Level Executives as judged by leader himself and as judged by his immediate subordinates and difference is found in authoritarian style.

10. In LIC, no significant difference is found in leadership styles at Middle Level Executives as judged by leader himself and as judged by his immediate subordinates and difference is found in authoritarian task orientation and nurrerant style.

11. In LIC, significant difference is found in leadership styles at Lower Level Executives as judged by leader himself and as judged by his immediate subordinates.

12. In CBB, significant difference is found in leadership styles at Higher Level Executives as judged by leader himself and as judged by his immediate subordinates and no difference in authoritarian style.

13. In CBB, no significant difference is found in leadership styles at Middle Level Executives as judged by leader himself and as judged by his immediate subordinates and difference in authoritarian and participative style.

14. In CBB, significant difference is found in leadership styles at Lower Level Executives as judged by leader himself and as judged by his immediate subordinates and no difference in authoritarian style.

(d) *The following are the major findings of the differences between leadership styles of employees of LIC and CBB self perception.*

15. No significant difference is found among different leadership styles at Higher Level Executives of LIC as well as CBB and difference in participative style.

16. No significant difference is found among different leadership styles at Middle Level Executives of LIC as well as CBB and differenc in participative style.

17 No significant difference is found among different leadership styles at Lower Level Executives of LIC as well as CBB and difference in task-orientation and nurturant styles.

(e) *The following are the major findings of differences between leadership styles of employees LIC and CBB as perceived by their subordinates.*

18. No significant difference is found among different leadership styles at Higher Level Executives of LIC as well as CBB and difference in authoritarians style.

19. No significant difference is found among different leadership styles at Middle Level Executives of LIC as well as CBB and difference in authuritarians styles.

20. No significant difference is found among different leadership styles at Lower Level Executives of LIC as well as CBB and difference in authoritarian, bureaucratic, nurturant styles

V. The following are the major findings of impacts of leadership on motivation.

21. There is significant difference between LIC and CBB employees in impact of leadership on motivation.
22. There is no significant difference between LIC and CBB Higher Level Executives in impact of leadership on motivation.
23. There is no significant difference between LIC and CBB Middle Level Executives in impact of leadership on motivation.
24. There is no significant difference between LIC and CBB Lower Level Executives in impact of leadership on motivation.
25. There is no significant difference between LIC and CBB Clerks in impact of leadership on motivation.
26. There is no significant difference between LIC Higher Level Executives and Middle Level Executives in impact of leadership on motivation.

27. There is significant difference between LIC Middle Level Executives and Lower Level Executives in impact of leadership on motivation.
28. There is significant difference between LIC Lower Level Executives and Clerks in impact of leadership on motivation.
29. There is no significant difference between CBB Higher Level Executives and Middle Level Executives in impact of leadership on motivation.
30. There is significant difference between CBB Middle Level Executives and Lower Level Executives in impact of leadership on motivation.
31. There is significant difference between CBB Lower Level Executives and Clerks in impact of leadership on motivation.
32. There is significant difference between LIC and CBB employees in impact of leadership on motivation under their high degree of motivation.
33. There is significant difference between LIC and CBB employees in impact of leadership on motivation under their low degree of motivation.
34. There is significant difference between LIC and CBB employees in impact of leadership on motivation under their moderate degree of motivation.

To sum up, the motivation and leadership are better among employees of LIC and CBB in Nellore district.

These findings are drawn from the opinions expressed by the employees of both the organisations at a given movement of time, though these findings are generally applicable to all the situations that would be prevailing similar to those under reference.

The results of the present research is used to design the works in the organisations under study, better and positive results can be expected.

CONCLUSIONS

From the overall analysis made by the researcher from empirical investigations presented in chapters III to VII about motivation and leadership in Life Insurance Corporation of India and Commercial bank branches reveals the following conclusions.

1. There are no proper perspectives about the significance of motivation among the employees of LIC and CBB. The employees with SEOP variables of LIC and CBB at different levels lack the proper perspectives of motivation and interlink with the leadership.
2. There is a mixed trend in the relationship of SEOP variables and leadership styles of the employees in LIC and CBB in terms of significance or insignificance.
3. There was no significant difference as perceived by the subordinates and leaders in LIC and CBB.
4. There was no significant proof that the leadership has any impact on motivation among the employees of LIC and CBB.

As such, the future policy related to man management in organizations is to be considered seriously in this backdrop.

SUGGESTIONS

Motivation and Leadership, are closely inter related and highly overlapping. Further, in all these man or woman is central to attain the needs and goals. Therefore, these issues cover a wide range of variables creating an incomprehensive picture while it is very difficult to adopt a specific package and approach to lead people with effective leadership and high motivation. Apart from this, there are other factors namely off the job factors which affect the behavior of the individual of his commitment and devotion to the job. Thus, the performance of an individual whether it is good or bad, is based finally on the out come of innumerable variables, umpteen factors and countless forces. Nevertheless, definitely unforeseen factors create an environment resulting in with bad relationship, low turnover, accidents, absenteeism, strikes and so on. Owing to these complexities a major suggestion to be made is that there should be an environment in which a spirit of 'give and take' policy by superiors and subordinates seriously addressed to and need to be developed.

The management either in LIC and CBB has to bestow its attention in eliminating differences related to either motivation or leadership due to the fact that there is a positive relationship among them. As such, management have to take care of identifying deficiencies and to avoid them on individual basis and organisational basis. It is because there cannot be uniform package that can be suggested to deal with all individuals in all organisations and at all times due to wide variance of their problems. A management further, should create such an environment of right leadership and high motivation where an individual would feel and realize his role and responsibility to fulfill the goals of self, as well as of the organisation.

EPILOGUE

The present study is confined to the hierarchical level of executives and clerical staff of LIC and CBB in Nellore district. Motivation is end product of the leadership. Leadership is the process of motivation. Improper leadership cannot create properly motivated human resource in organisations. What all the efforts and resource employed for improving the efficiency and effectiveness of organisation will goes in vein without competent leadership. Thus, there is a dire need to know the key factors for improving the leadership and consequently the motivation of the employees. This demands different studies covering various types of organisations in different cultural contexts. Despite the literature and research findings available at command of the theoreticians and practitioners of leadership, at an enigma, puzzling all those involved in the process. The function of motivation is leadership, the process of leadership is motivation.

Further studies, thus, should cover a comparison between service sector organisations like Hospitals, Universities, Private and Public sector and Manufacturing organisations taking both the 'on the job' and 'off the job' factors in different cultural settings in order to know the variables which have higher influence on motivation and leadership.

COPY OF SCHEDULE

I. PERSONAL PROFILE :

Age	:	Years	( )
Designation	:		
Experience (in years)	:		
Educational qualifications:			
Economic Status	:	Lower Middle Class	( )
		Middle Class	( )
		Upper Class	( )

II. MOTIVATION

The following statements have been designed to know your opinion on some factors relating to 'Motivation'. Please read each statement and decide as to what extent you agree or disagree with the statement and show your response by drawing a circle around one of the five responses. The responses are measured on a five point scale given below:

SA = Strongly Agree,
A = Agree,
MA = Moderately Agree,
D = Disagree,
SD = Strongly Disagree

1.	I want to dominate people working in my organization	SA	A	MA	D	SD
2.	I want to influence people	SA	A	MA	D	SD
3.	I want to control people	SA	A	MA	D	SD
4.	I want to exercise power	SA	A	MA	D	SD
5.	I like to direct others towards goals	SA	A	MA	D	SD

	Statement					
6.	I like to have social contacts with people working in the organization	SA	A	MA	D	SD
7.	I like companionship with others	SA	A	MA	D	SD
8.	I seek other's support	SA	A	MA	D	SD
9.	I like to extend support to others	SA	A	MA	D	SD
10.	I like to develop meaningful relationships with others	SA	A	MA	D	SD
11.	I prefer frequent interactions with co-workers	SA	A	MA	D	SD
12.	I like challenging work	SA	A	MA	D	SD
13.	I would like to shoulder responsibility	SA	A	MA	D	SD
14.	I would like to know how well I am doing	SA	A	MA	D	SD
15.	I would like to develop skills and abilities	SA	A	MA	D	SD
16.	My work is challenging	SA	A	MA	D	SD
17.	I want to get rewards by fulfilling the challenging work	SA	A	MA	D	SD
18.	I will withdraw from work if expected reward is not given	SA	A	MA	D	SD
19.	I always compare my performance with my colleagues' performance	SA	A	MA	D	SD
20.	I have enough skills to do my work	Yes / No				
21.	Skills of my colleagues are: *(Please select a, b, or c)*					
	a) Equal to me	SA	A	MA	D	SD
	b) More than me	SA	A	MA	D	SD
	c) Less than me	SA	A	MA	D	SD
22.	I always compare my performance with my colleagues	Yes / No				
23.	My performance is: *(Please select a, b or c)*					
	a) Equal to my colleagues	SA	A	MA	D	SD
	b) More than my colleagues	SA	A	MA	D	SD
	c) Less than my colleagues	SA	A	MA	D	SD

24. I always compare my pay with my performance — Yes / No

25. My pay is : *(Please select a, b or c)*

a) Equal to my performance	SA	A	MA	D	SD
b) More than my performance	SA	A	MA	D	SD
c) less than my performance	SA	A	MA	D	SD

26. Performance and rewards are strictly matched in the organization — Yes / No

27. My promotions are : *(Please select a, b or c)*

a) Equal to my colleagues	SA	A	MA	D	SD
b) More than my colleagues	SA	A	MA	D	SD
c) Less than my colleagues	SA	A	MA	D	SD

28. All in all we are enjoying equal benefits and comforts in the organization — Yes/No

29. I have reasonable amount of salary and fringe benefits for my job	SA	A	MA	D	SD
30. I have security in my job	SA	A	MA	D	SD
31. I have an opportunity to talk with others in my job.	SA	A	MA	D	SD
32. I have an opportunity to develop close friendship in my job	SA	A	MA	D	SD
33. I have a feeling of self-esteem in my job	SA	A	MA	D	SD
34. I have prestige in my job	SA	A	MA	D	SD
35. I have authority connected to my job	SA	A	MA	D	SD
36. I have an opportunity to participate in the setting of goals	SA	A	MA	D	SD
37. I have independence in my job	SA	A	MA	D	SD
38. I have an opportunity for personal growth and development	SA	A	MA	D	SD
39. I have self-fulfillment in my job	SA	A	MA	D	SD
40 I have worth while accomplishment in my job.	SA	A	MA	D	SD

III. LEADER'S SELF PERCEPTION

Below are given some statements regarding the Behaviour of a leader. Please judge to what extent they are true or false for you are in the leading role. Put a circle around one of the five responses against each statement.

QT – Quite True

T – True

D – Doubtful

F – False

QF – Quite False

	Statement					
1.	I maintain partnership in the group	QT	T	D	F	QF
2.	I help my subordinates in their career planning.	QT	T	D	F	QF
3.	I keep crucial information to myself.	QT	T	D	F	QF
4.	I help my subordinates to grow up and assume responsibility.	QT	T	D	F	QF
5.	I explain to my subordinates what is expected from them and what they can expect from me .	QT	T	D	F	QF
6.	I make my subordinates feel free and even to disagree with me.	QT	T	D	F	QF
7.	I interact with my subordinates as if they are equal	QT	T	D	F	QF
8.	I take special care to get the work done with top priority.	QT	T	D	F	QF
9.	I maintain fair but impersonal relationship in the group.	QT	T	D	F	QF
10.	I go by joint decisions of the group.	QT	T	D	F	QF
11.	I maintain high standard of performance	QT	T	D	F	QF
12.	I guide my subordinates to feel the sense of responsibility	QT	T	D	F	QF
13.	I think that if clear-cut job descriptions are available, there will be less conflict in the organization.	QT	T	D	F	QF

14. I help my subordinates to increase their knowledge on the job	QT	T	D	F	QF
15. I openly show affection to those subordinates who work hard	QT	T	D	F	QF
16. I give as much responsibility as my subordinates can handle	QT	T	D	F	QF
17. I consider seniority as a time-tested criterion for promotion	QT	T	D	F	QF
18. I see that subordinates work to their maximum capacity.	QT	T	D	F	QF
19. I grant full freedom and autonomy to my subordinates so that they can work hard.	QT	T	D	F	QF
20. I favour that the area of responsibility should be clearly demarcated according to rank and positions.	QT	T	D	F	QF
21. I inform my subordinates how well they are doing their job.	QT	T	D	F	QF
22. I do not tolerate any interference from my subordinates.	QT	T	D	F	QF
23. I am alert all the time as there are many people who may pull me down	QT	T	D	F	QF
24. I never question the well–established ways of doing things in this organization.	QT	T	D	F	QF
25. I believe that top boss makes major decisions and implements them.	QT	T	D	F	QF
26. I rule with an iron hand to get the work done.	QT	T	D	F	QF
27. I want have full power and control over my subordinates.	QT	T	D	F	QF
28. I categorize my subordinates as good and bad	QT	T	D	F	QF
29. I am a friendly type.	QT	T	D	F	QF
30. I have affection for my subordinates.	QT	T	D	F	QF

IV. SUBORDINATES' PERCEPTION ON SUPERIOR LEADERSHIP STYLES

Below are given some statements regarding the behaviour of a leader. Please judge to what extent they are true or false about your superior when you are in subordinate's role. Put a circle around one of the five responses against each statement.

QT – Quite True

T – True

D – Doubtful

F – False

QF – Quite False

1. He maintains partnership in the group. QT T D F QF
2. He helps us in our career planning. QT T D F QF
3. He keeps crucial information to himself alone. QT T D F QF
4. He helps us to grow up and assume responsibility. QT T D F QF
5. He explains to us what he expect from us and what we can expect from him QT T D F QF
6. He makes us feel free even to disagree with him. QT T D F QF
7. He interacts with us as if we are equal. QT T D F QF
8. He takes special care to get the work done with top priority. QT T D F QF
9. He maintains fair but impersonal relationship in the group QT T D F QF
10. He goes by the joint decisions of the group QT T D F QF
11. He maintains high standard of performance. QT T D F QF
12. He believe that we acquire sense of responsibility under the care and guidance of a good leader. QT T D F QF
13. He thinks that if clear-cut job descriptions are available, there will be less conflict in an organization. QT T D F QF

14. He believes that one can really grow up by learning to do a job well. QT T D F QF
15. He openly show affection to those subordinates who work hard. QT T D F QF
16. He gives as much responsibility as we can handle. QT T D F QF
17. He considers seniority as a time tested criterion for promotion. QT T D F QF
18 He sees that we work to our capacity. QT T D F QF
19 He grants full freedom and autonomy to us so that we can work hard. QT T D F QF
20. He favours that the area of responsibility should be clearly demarcated according to rank and positions. QT T D F QF
21. He informs us how well we are doing our job. QT T D F QF
22. He does not tolerate any interference from us QT T D F QF
23. He believes that if he is not alert all the time there are many people who may pull him down. QT T D F QF
24 He never questions the procedures of doing things in this organization. QT T D F QF
25. He believes that the top boss makes major decisions and implements them. QT T D F QF
26. He rules with an iron hand to get the work done QT T D F QF
27. He want to have full power and control over us. QT T D F QF
28. He categorizes us as good and bad. QT T D F QF
29. He is friendly type QT T D F QF
30. He has affection for us. QT T D F QF

V. IMPACT OF LEADERSHIP ON MOTIVATION OF SUBORDINATE

1. My superior motivates me to do the job well SA A MA D SD

2. My superior influences me to acquire new knowledge and skills. SA A MA D SD
3. My superior provides me solace in the calamities I face. SA A MA D SD
4. My superior fights with the organisation superiors to provide the benefits due to me SA A MA D SD
5. My superior understands my psychology SA A MA D SD
6. My superior gives proper instructions SA A MA D SD
7. My superior provides the confidence to me that I can fulfill my ambition in life SA A MA D SD
8. My superior provides the needed security on my job SA A MA D SD
9. My superior never feels the envy for my growth SA A MA D SD
10. My superior visits my residence often. SA A MA D SD
11. My superior attends all the functions to which I invite him. SA A MA D SD
12. My superior dines with me in my house SA A MA D SD
13. My superior knows about the names and details of my family members SA A MA D SD
14. My superior enquires about the welfare of my family SA A MA D SD
15. My superior evinces interest in my personal problems SA A MA D SD
16. My superior helps overcome the crisis I face SA A MA D SD
17. My superior discuss his problems with me SA A MA D SD
18. My superior accepts my suggestions often SA A MA D SD
19. My superior loves me SA A MA D SD
20. My superior protects me whenever needed SA A MA D SD
21. My superior delegates me the required power to undertake my job SA A MA D SD

22. My superior communicates with me with the spirit of understanding	SA	A	MA	D	SD
23. My superior provides me good moral support.	SA	A	MA	D	SD
24. My superior is friendly with me.	SA	A	MA	D	SD
25. My superior is compassionate towards me.	SA	A	MA	D	SD
26. My superior maintains proper discipline.	SA	A	MA	D	SD
27. My superior inculcates good competitive spirit.	SA	A	MA	D	SD
28. My superior forgives me for the mistakes committed by me	SA	A	MA	D	SD
29. My superior is visionary in the departmental tasks.	SA	A	MA	D	SD
30. My superior is not egoist.	SA	A	MA	D	SD
31. My superior does not suffer from pride.	SA	A	MA	D	SD
32. My superior does not suffer from greed.	SA	A	MA	D	SD
33. My superior does not suffer from anger.	SA	A	MA	D	SD
34. My superior is not cunning in his transactions.	SA	A	MA	D	SD
35. My superior is a role model to me.	SA	A	MA	D	SD
36. My superior extracts work with tact.	SA	A	MA	D	SD
37. My superior handles my grievances properly.	SA	A	MA	D	SD
38. My superior helps overcome the shyness.	SA	A	MA	D	SD
39. My superior helps overcome the laziness.	SA	A	MA	D	SD
40. My superior likes sincerity.	SA	A	MA	D	SD

BIBLIOGRAPHY

BOOKS

Andrew J Dubrin; *"Leadership: Research Findings Practice and Skills"* Rochester Institute of Technology, Mifftin Company, Boston Toronto, Geneva – 1998.

Apple White, Philip B. *"Organisational Behaviour,"* Engle Wood Cliffs, Prentice-Hall, New Jersey, 1965.

Argyris C. Schon D *"Theory in Practice,"* Jossy – Bass, San-Francisco, California, 1974.

Atikinson, J.W. *"An Introduction to Motivation"* D. Van Nostrand Company, 1969.

Aswathappa, K., "Organisational Behaviour" Himalaya Pulblishing House, Bangalore, 1997.

Bass, B. M.*"Leadership, Psychology and Organizational Behaviour"*, Harper, New York, 1960.

Blake, R.R. and *"The Managerial Grid,"* Gulf Publishing, Mouton S.J. Company, Houston, Taxaus, 1964.

Brown, J.S. *"The Motivation to Behaviour "* Mc Graw Hill New Yark, 1959.

Burns J. M. *"Leadership,"* Harper and Row, New York, 1978.

Campbell, D.P. *Campbell Leadership Index Manual,* National Computer System, 1991.

Carter, L.F. *"Leadership and Small Group Behaviour,"* in M. Sheriff and M.O. Wilson, eds. "Group Relations at the Crossroads," Harper, 1953.

Carnarius, Stanely E. : *"Motivating Managers"*. Opinion Research Corporation, August, 1962.

Chester I. Bernard *"The Functions of the Executive,"* Harvard University Press, Cambridge, 1946.

Cofer, C.N. & Appley. M.H. *"Motivation Theory and Research"*, New Yark Wiley, 1967.

Chris Argyris *"Executive Leadership,"* Harper and Brothers Publishers, New York, 1953.

Daniel Katz et. al. *"Productivity, Supervision and Morale in Office Situation,"* Survey Research Centre, University of Michigan, Ann Arbor, 1950.

David A. Whetten and *"Developing Management Skills,"* Kim S. Cameron Harper Collins, New York, 1991.

Douglas McGregor *"The Human Side of Enterprise,"* McGraw–Hill International Book Company, New York, 1960.

Fiedler, F.E. *"A Theory of Leadership Effectiveness,"* McGraw Hill, New York, 1967.

Filley, A.C., House, R.J. *"Managerial Process and Organizational* and Kerr, S. *Behaviour,"* 2nd Ed. Scott, Foresman, 1976.

Gelleraman, S.W. *"Management by Motivation"* American Management Association, New York, 1963.

Gary A. Yukl *"Leadership in Organisations,"* 2nd ed. Prentice Hall, Englewood Cliffs, New Jersey, 1989.

George R. Terry *"Principles of Management,"* Richard, D. Irwin, Inc. Home Wood, Illinois, 1968.

Gibb, C.A. *"Leadership"* in Hand Book of Social Psychology Edited by Lindzey, G. and Aronson, Vol.4, Addison-Wesley, Mass, 1969.

Haiman, F.S. *"Group Leadership and Democratic Action,"* Houghton Mifflin, Boston, 1951.

Harold Koontz and *"Essentials of Management,"* Tata Cyril O' Donnell McGraw-Hill Publishing Company, New Delhi, 1978.

Harold Koontz and Heinz Weihrich *"Essentials of Management,"* 5th Edition, McGraw Hill Series in Management, New York, 1990.

Henry Mintzberg *"The Nature of Managerial Work,"* Prentice Hall, Englewood Cliffs, New Jersey, 1980.

Herbert G. Hicks and *"The Management of Organizations,"* C. Roy Gullet 3rd edition, McGraw-Hill Series in Management, New York.

Henry Fayol *"General and Industrial Management,"* Pitman and Sons, London, 1949.

Herzberg, F. et. al *"The Motivation to Work"*, John Willey, New York, 1953.

Hingar Asha *"Leadership Styles and Job Satisfaction,"* Printwell Publishers, Jaipur, 1986.

Hodge B.J. and *"Management of Organisational Johnson H.J.Behaviour,"* John Wiley and Sons, New York, 1970.

House R.J. and Dessler G. in Hunt J.G. and Larson, L. (Eds) *"The Path-Goal Theory of Leadership"* Contingency Approaches to Leadership, Souther Illionois, University Press, 1974.

Hunt, J.W. *"Managing People at Work,"* 2nd Edition, McGraw-Hill, New York, 1986.

Ivancevich, Donnelly and Gibson *"Management Principles and Functions,"* 4th edition, All India Traveller Book seller, Delhi, 1991.

Ivancevich, Szilagyi and Wallance *"Organisation Behaviour and Performance,"* (Adopted from Dr. M.J. Mathew, *"Organisation: Theory and Behaviour,"* RBSA Publishers, Jaipur, 1993)

James M. Kouzes and Posner *"The Leadership Challenge: How to Barry Z. Get Extraordinary Things Done in Organizations,"* Jossey-Bass, San Francisco, 1987.

John P. Kotter *"A Force for Change: How Leadership Differs from Management,"* The Free Press, New York, 1990; (Warren Bennis, *"An Invented Life: Reflections on Leadership and Change,"* Addison-Wesley, Reading, Mass., 1993)...

John R.P. French and Raven *"The Basis of Social Power,"* in studies Betram in Social Power. D. Cart Wright, University of Michigan Press, Ann Arbor, 1959.

Kakabadse, Andrew *"Leadership for the Third Millennium," Essence of Leadership*, International Thompson Publishing, 1998.

Kakar, S. *"Personality and Authority in Work,"* Somaiya Publications, Bombay, 1974.

Kalra H.K. *"Leadership Styles of Executives in Indian Enterprises,"* unpublished Research Report, Punjab Agricultural University, Ludhiana, 1980.

Kapila, P.D. *"Leadership Styles in Public Sector"* in 'Leadership and Managerial Effectiveness', Narayan, B. (Ed) Janaki Prakashan, New Delhi, 1987.

Katz. D.N. , Maccoby and Morse *"Productivity, Supervision, and Morale in an Office Situation,"* Survey Research Center, Institute for Social Research, University of Michigan, Ann Arber, Michigan, 1950.

Keith Davis *"Human Behaviour at Work,"* Tata McGraw-Hill Company Ltd., New Delhi, 1975.

Koontz and O' Donnel *"Management,"* McGraw-Hill International Book Company, 1st Printing, New York, 1984.

Koontz, H. and Weihrich, H. *"Management,"* 9th Edition, McGraw-Hill Company, Yew York, 1989.

Krech, D., Crutchfield, *"Individual in Society,"* McGraw-Hill, R.S. and Ballachey, E,L. New York, 1962.

Krech, E. and Crutchfield, R.S. *"Theory and Problems of Social Psychology,"*, McGraw Hill, New York, 1948.

Litwin, G.H. & Stinger *"Motivation and Organization Climate"*

R.A., Division of Research H.B. School, Boston, 1968.

Max Weber cited in S.N. Eisenstadt, *"Max Weber: On Charisma and Institution Building,"* University of Chicago Press, Chicago, 1968.

Maslow, A.H. *"A Theory of Meta Motivation : The Biological Rooting of the Value of Life"*; I humanistic psychology, 1967.

Maslow, A.H. *"Motivation and Personality"* Harper, New York, 1954.

Myers C.A. *"Industrial Relations in India,"* Asia Publishing House, Bombay, 1960.

Nanus. B. *"Visionary Leadership,"* Free Press, New York, 1992.

Noel M. Tichy *"The Leadership Engine: How Winning Companies Build Leaders at Every Level,"* Harper Collins Publishers, Inc., New York, 1997.

Ordway Tead *"The Art of Leadership,"* McGraw Hill Book Company, Inc. New York, 1953.

Ouchi, W.G. *"Theory Z: How American Business Can Meet the Japanese Challenge,"* Addison-Wesley, 1981.

Peter Drucker *"Practice of Management,"* Allied Publishers, New Delhi, 1970.

Punekar S.D. and Savur M.G., *"Management - White Collar Relations,* "Popular Prakashan, Bombay, 1969.

Ralph M. Stogdill *"Handbook of Leadership: A Survey of Theory and Research,"* The Free Press, New York, 1974.

Rensis Likert *"New Pattern of Management,"* McGraw-Hill, New York, 1961.

Rensis Likert *"The Human Organization,"* McGraw Hill, New York, 1967.

Roach, C.F. and Behling, O., *"Functionalism: Basis for an AlternativeApproach to the Study of Leadership,"* in *Leadership and Managers* by J.G. Hunt (ed.), Pergamon, New York, 1984.

Robbins, S.P. *"Organisational Behaviour: Concepts and Controversies,"* Engle Wood cliffs, Prentice Hall, New Jersey, 1979.

Robert J. House *"A 1976 Theory of Charismatic Leadership,"* in J. G.Hunt and L. L. Larson (eds), *"Leadership: The Cutting Edge"* Southern Illinois University Press, Carbondale, 1977.

Robert R. Blake and Jane S. Mouton Houston, *"The Managerial Grid,"* Gulf Publishing, 1978.

S.P. Robbins *"Organisational Behaviour,"* Prentice Hall Inc., Englewood Cliffs, 1979.

Sharma, A.K. *"Motivational Dynamic"* Rawat Publication, Jaipur, 1990.

Shartle, C.L. *"Studies in Naval Leadership,"* in H. Guetzkow Groups, *"Leadership and Men,"* Carnegie Press, Pittsburgh, 1951.

Siegel, J. P. *"A Study of the Relationship among Organizational Factors, Personality Traits, Job and Leadership Attitudes," Dissertation Abstracts*, 29 (1969).

Sinha, J.B.P. *"The Nurturant Task-Behaviour,"* Concept Publishing Company, New Delhi, 1980.

Steers R.M. and Porter, L.W, *"Motivation and work Behaviour"* Mc Graw Hill Book Co., New York,1952.

Stogdill, R.M. *"Hand Book of Leadership: A Survey of Theory and Research,"* Free Press, New York, 1974.

Stogdill, R.M. *"Individual Behaviour and Group Achievement,"* Oxford University Press, New York, 1959.

Stogdill, R.M. *"Managers, Employees, Organisations,"* Bureau of Business Research, Ohio State University, Columbus, 1965.

Szilagyi and Wallace *"Organisational Behaviour and Performance,"* Richard D. Irwin, Inc. Homewood, Illinois, 1968.

Tichy,N.M. and Devanna,M.A., *"The Transformational Leader,"*Wiley, New York, 1986.

V.S.P. Rao and P.S. Narayana , *"Organisation Theory and Behaviour,"* Vikas Publishing House, New Delhi, 1986.

Vroom V.H. and Yetton P.W., *"Leadership and Decision Making,"* University of Pittsburgh Press, 1973.

Vroom, V. *"Some Personality Determinants of the Effects of Participation,"* Prentice Hall, Englewood Cliffs, N.J., 1960.

Vroom, V.H. *"The Search for a Theory of Leadership in Contemporary Management: Issues and View Points,"* Ed. Joseph W. McGuire, Englewood Cliffs, N.J., Prentice-Hall, 1974.

Vroom V.H. *"Work and Motivation"* John Wilay and Sons, Inc. New York, 1964.01Yetton P.W.

W.J. Reddin *"Managerial Effectiveness,"* McGraw-Hill, New York, 1970.

Yukl, G.A *"Leader Personality and Situational Variables as Co-Determinants of Leader Behavior," Dissertation Abstract*, 29 (1968).

PERIODICALS

Ansari, M.A. *"Need for Nurturant-Task Leaders in India: Some empirical evidence," Management and Labour Studies*, 11,1, (1986), pp.26-36.

Argyris, C. *"Theories in Action that Inhibit Individual Leaving," American Psychologist*, Vol.31, 1976, pp.638-654.

Baumgartel, H. *"Leadership, Motivations and Attitudes in Research Laboratories," Journal of Social Issues*, 12, (1956), pp.24-31.

Bennis, W. G. *"Leadership Theory and Administrative Behaviour: The Problem of Authority," Administrative Science Quarterly*, Vol.4, 1959, pp. 259-269.

Bernard M. Bass *"From Transactional to Transformational Leadership: Learning to Share the Vision," Organizational Dynamics*, Winter, 1990, pp.19-31.

Bhusan, L.I. *"Leadership Performance as related to Age, Education, Residence and Sex," Indian Journal of Social Work*, July, Volume 1, (1968), pp.193-196.

Cattell, R.B. and Stice, G.F.*"Four formulae for Selecting Leaders on the basis of Personality," Human Relations*, 7 (1954).

Charles C. Manz and Henry P.Sims, Jr. *"Super Leadership: Beyond the Myth of Heroic Leadership," Organizational Dynamics*, Spring 1991, P.18.

Conger, Jam. and Kanungo, R. *"Toward A Behavioural Theory of Charismatic Leadership in Organizational Setting," Academy of Management Review*, Vol.12, No.4, October 1987, pp.637-648.

Wilkinson *"Dynamics"*, *Winter* 1984, pp.58-67.

Elhance, D.N. and *Lok* Agarwal, R.D., *"Delegation of Authority," Udyog*, 6 (1973).

Evans, M.G. *"The Effect of Supervisory Behaviour on the Path-Goal Relationship,"Organizational Behaviour and Human Performance*, 5 (1970), pp.277-297.

Fiedler, F.E. *"Style or Circumstance: The Leadership Enigma," Psychology Today*, March, 1969, p.39

Fleishman, E.A. *"Leadership Climate, Human Relations Training, and Supervisory Behaviour," Personnel Psychology*, Vol.6, No.2, Summer, 1953, pp.205-222.

Fleishman, E.A. and Simmons, J., *"Relationship between Leadership Patterns and Effectiveness ratings among Israeli foreman," Personnel Psychology*, 23 (1970), pp.169-172.

Getzels, J.S. and Guba E.G., *"Social Behaviour and the Administrative Process," School Review*, 55 (1957).

Gheselli, E.E. *"Management Talent," American Psychologist*, Vol.18, Oct, 1963, pp.631-642.

Gore, W.J. and Silander, F.S, *"A Bibliographical Essay on Decision Making," Administrative Science Quarterly*, Vol.6, 1959, pp.121-129.

Graham, W.K. *"Leader Behavior, Esteem for Least-Preferred Co-Worker, and Group Performance,"* American Psychological Association, 1968, pp.33-40.

Habibullah, A.H.M. and Sinha, J.B.P., *"Motivational Climate and Leadership Styles," Vikalpa*, 5 (1980).

Harding, L. W., *"Twenty-One Varieties of Educational Leadership," Educational Leadership*, 6 (1949), pp. 299-302.

Harris, E.F. and E.A. Fleishman, *"Human Relations Training and the Stability of Leadership Patterns," Journal of Applied Psychology*, 39 (1955).

Hemphill, J.K. *"The Leader and his Group," Journal of Educational Research*, 28 (1949).

Hollander, E.P., and Jullian J.W., *"Contemporary Trends in the Analysis of Leadership Processes," Psychological Bulletin*, 71 (1996) pp.387-391.

House R.J. "*A Path-Goal Theory of Leadership Effectiveness,*" *Administrative Science Quarterly*, Vol.16, Sep.1971, pp.321-338.

House R.J. "*A Path-Goal Theory of Leader Effectiveness,*" *Administrative Science Quarterly*, September 1971, pp.321-338, and R.J. House and T.R.Mitchel, "*Path-Goal Theory of Leadership,*" *Journal of Contemporary Business*, Autumn, 1974, p.86.

James J. Cribbin "*Effective Managerial Leadership,*" American Management Association, 1972, p.9.

James Owen "*The Uses of Leadership Theory,*" *Michigan Business Review*, Vol.25, No.1, January, 1973, pp.13-19.

Jennings, E.E. "*The Anatomy of Leadership,*" *Management of Personnel Quarterly*, Vol.1, Autumn, 1961, p.2.

Joseph P.M. and Kesavan R., "*A Comparative Study of Leader Behaviour in Public and Private Sectors in India,*" *Indian Manager*, April-June 1977.

Karmel, B. "*Leadership: A Challenge to Traditional Research Methods and Assumptions,*" *Academy of Management Review*, Vol.3, 1978, pp.475-482.

Kidd, J.S., and Christy, R.T., "*Supervisory Procedures and Work TeamProductivity,*" *Journal of Applied Psychology*, 45, (1961), pp.388-392.

Korman, A.K. "*Consideration, Initiating Structure and Organizational Criteria: A review,*" *Personnel Psychology*, 19 (1966).

Kumar, Usha and Singh, K.K., "*The Inter-Personal Construct System of the Indian Manager: A determinant of Organizational Behavior,*" *Indian Journal of Psychology*, 51 (1976), pp.275-278, (p.288).

Kurt Lewin, Ronald lippitt and Ralph K. White, "*Patterns of Aggressive Behaviour in Experimentally Created Social Climates,*" *Journal of Social Psychology*, Vol.10, No.2, May, 1939, pp.271-299.

Levine, S. "*An Approach to Constructive Leadership,*" *Journal of Sociological Issues*, 5 (1949), 46-53.

Lewin, K., Lippitt, R. and White, R.K. "*Patterns of Aggressive Behaviour in Experimentally Created 'Social Climates',*" *Journal of Social Psychology*, Vol.10, 1939, pp.271-299.

Lokhande M.R. and Singh S.N."*Leadership Patterns and Social Change,*"*Journal of the Council of Social Development*, Volume 7, No.1, March 1977, pp.14-19.

Maier, N.F.R. *"The Quality of Group Decisions as Influenced by the Discussion Leader," Human Relations*, 6, (1950), pp.161-173.

Manisha Agarwal and G.C. Agarwal *"Relationship of Middle Managers' Power Styles with their Participativeness at the Work Place," Indian Journal of Industrial Relations*, Volume 30, No.3, January 1995, pp.278-288.

McCurely, H.G., and Eber, H.W. *"Democratic Versus Authoritarian: A Further Investigation of Group Problem Solving," Journal of Personality*, 22, (1953), pp.258-269.

Merton, R.K. *"The Social Nature of Leadership," American Journal of Nursing*, 69, 1969, pp.2614-2618.

Michael J. Marquart and Dean W. Engel *"HRD Competencies for a Shrinking World," Training and Development*, May 1993, pp.62-64.

Morris, W.T. and Seeman, M. *"The Problem of Leadership: An Interdisciplinary Approach," American Journal of Sociology*, 56 (1950), pp.149-155.

Mullen, J.H. *"Differential Leadership Modes and Productivity in a Large Organization," Academy of Management Journal*, 3 (1965), pp.107-126.

Munson, C.E. *"Style and Structure in Supervision," Journal of Education for Social Work*, 17, 1981 pp.65-72.

Neelama Varma *"A Test of Implicit Personality Theories of Leadership," Indian Journal of Industrial Relations*, Volume 22, No.2, Oct, 1986, pp.189-198.

Nitish De *"Dilemmas of Indian Managers,"* Management in Government, July-September 1974.

Noel M. Tichy and Mary Anne Devanna, *"The Transformational Leader," Training and Development Journal*, July 1986, pp.30-32.

Omer Bin Sayeed *"Conflict Management Styles: Relationship with Leadership Styles and Moderating Effect of Esteem for Coworker," Indian Journal of Industrial Relations*, Vol.26, No.1, July 1990, pp.28-52.

Pigors, P. *"Types of Leaders in Group Work," Sociology and Social Research*, 21 (1936), pp.3-17.

Rabindra M. Kanungo and Sasi Misra *"Managerial Resourcefulness: A Reconceptualization of Management Skills," Human Relations*, December 1992, pp.1311-1332.

Rajinder Kaur *"Managerial Styles in the Public Sector," Indian Journal of Industrial Relations,* Volume 28, No.4, April, 1993, pp.363-367.

Ralph M. Stogdill *"Personal Factors Associated with Leadership: A Survey of the Literature," Journal of Psychology,* Jan.1948, pp.35-71.

Rama J. Joshi *"Managerial Effectiveness: As Perceived by Chief Executives," Indian Journal of Industrial Relations,* Volume 27, No.1, July 1991, pp.69-78.

Rambo, W.W. *"The Construction and analysis of a Leadership Behavior Rating form," Journal of Applied Psychology,* 42 (1958), pp.409-415.

Reddin J. William. *"The 3-D Management Style Theory," Training and Development Journal,* April 1967, pp.8-17.

Robert L. Katz *"The Skills of an Effective Administrator," Harvard Business Review,* September-October 1974, pp.90-102.

Robert Tannenbaum and Warren H. *"How to choose a Leadership Pattern," Harvard Business Review* (March–Schmidt, April 1958), pp.95-101,

Heinz Weihrich, *"How to Change a Leadership pattern,"* Management Review (April 1979) pp.26-28, 37-40.

Sanderson, D. and Nafe, R.W., *"Studies in Rural Leadership,"* Publ. Amer. Social. Soc., 23 (1929), pp.163-175.

Selvadurai S. *"Leadership in the Co-operatives: Some perceptions of Leaders," Indian management,* July 1997, pp.40-45.

Sequeira, C.E. *"Functions of a Supervisor,"* Indian Journal of Applied Psychology, 1, (1962), pp.46-54.

Shaw, M.E. *"A Comparison of two types of Leadership in Various Communication Nets," Journal of Abnormal and Social Psychology,* 50, (1955), pp.127-134.

Singh, A.P. & Das, G.S. *"Management Style of Indian Manager: A profile,"* ASCI *Journal of Management,* September 1977.

Singh, P. *"Leadership Process and its Impact on Productivity, Satisfaction and Work Commitment," Decision,* Volume 6, 1979, pp.259-269.

Sinha J.B.P. *"The Authoritative Leadership: A Style of Effective Management," Indian Journal of Industrial Relations,* 11 (1976), pp.381-389.

Sinha, J.B.P. and Chowdary, G.P., *"Perception of Subordinates as a Moderator of Leadership Effectiveness,"* A.N.S. Institute of Social Studies, Patna, 1979 (mimeographed).

Sinha,T.N. and Sinha,J.B.P., *"Styles of Leadership and their effects on Group Productivity,"* A.N.S. Institute of Social Studies, Patna, 1977 (mimeographed).

Skinner, Elizabeth, W. *"Relationships between Leadership Behaviour Patterns and Organizational Situational Variables," Personnel Psychology*, 22 (1969), pp.489-494.

Spector, P. and Suttell Barbara, J., *"Research on the specific leader behaviour patterns most effective in influencing group performance,"* American Institute for Research, Washington, D.C., 1956.

Steven Kerr and John M. Jermier , *"Substitutes for Leadership: Their Meaning and Measurement," Organisational Behaviour and Human Performance*, December 1978, pp.375-403.

Steven Kerr, Chester, A. Schniesheim, Charles J. Murphy, and Ralph. M. Stogdill. *"Toward a Contingency Theory of* Leadership *based upon the Consideration and Initiating Structure Literature," Organizational Behaviour and Human Performance*, August 1974, pp.62-82.

Stogdill, R.M. *"Personal Factors Associated with Leadership: A Survey of Literature," Journal of Psychology*, Vol.25, 1948, pp.35-71.

Syed Vazith Hussain *"Leadership Styles in Small Scale Industries," The Indian Journal of Commerce*, Vol.55, No.3, July-September 2002, pp.45-54.

Tannenbaum, R. and Schmidt, W.H., *"How to Choose a Leadership Pattern," Harvard Business Review*, May-June, 1973. pp.162-175, 178-180.

Thiagarajan, K.M. and Deep, S.D. *"A Study of Supervisor Subordinate Satisfaction in four Cultures," Journal of Social Psychology*, 82 (1970), 173-180.

Tosi, H. *"A Re-Examination of Personality as a determinant of the effects of Participation," Personnel Psychology*, 23 (1970), pp.91-99.

V. Ravichandran and D. Nagabrahmam, *"Leadership in a Transitory Environment," Indian Journal of Industrial Relations*, Volume 32, No.4, April 1997, pp.423-435.

Venkatapathy R. *"Perception of Top Management Leadership Styles and Climate: A Study of Public and Private Executives," Indian Journal of Industrial Relations*, Volume-25, No.3, January 1990.

Vroom, V., & Mann, F. *"Leader Authoritarianism and Employee Attitudes," Personnel Psychology*, 13 (1960), pp.125-140.

Weschler, J.R., Kahane, M., and Tannenbaum, R., "*Job Satisfaction, Productivity, and Morale: A Case Study,*" *Occupational Psychology*,26, (1952), pp.1-14.

Wexley, K.N., Singh, J.P. and Yukl, G.A. "*Subordinate Personality as Moderator of the Effects of Participation in three types of Appraisal Interviews,*" *Journal of Applied Psychology*, 58 (1973), pp.54-59.